✧ *Companions for the Journey* ✧

Praying with
Teilhard de Chardin

✧ *Companions for the Journey* ✧

Praying with Teilhard de Chardin

by
James W. Skehan, SJ

Saint Mary's Press
Christian Brothers Publications
Winona, Minnesota

✧ *To my parents,* ✧
James William and Mary Effie Coffey Skehan;
my brothers, Joseph B. and Francis A.;
and sisters, Mary Watson, Teresa, RSM, and Marie Cooney;
my Jesuit brothers;
and all others who love the world

 Genuine recycled paper with 10% post-consumer waste.
Printed with soy-based ink.

The publishing team for this book included Stephan Nagel and Mary Duerson, development editors; James H. Gurley, production editor and typesetter; Cären Yang, cover designer; Sam Thiewes, illustrator; produced by the graphics division of Saint Mary's Press.

The acknowledgments continue on page 123.

Printed in the United States of America

Printing: 9 8 7 6 5 4 3 2 1

Year: 2009 08 07 06 05 04 03 02 01

ISBN 0-88489-656-0

Library of Congress Cataloging-in-Publication Data

Skehan, James W.
    Praying with Teilhard de Chardin / by James W. Skehan.
        p. cm. — (Companions for the journey)
Includes bibliographical references.
    ISBN 0-88489-656-0 (pbk.)
1. Teilhard de Chardin, Pierre. 2. Catholic Church—Prayer-books and devotions—English. I. Title. II. Series.
    BX4705.T39 S56 2000
    242—dc21
                                                    00-011562

✧ Contents ✧

✧ Foreword ✧

Companions for the Journey

Just as food is required for human life, so are companions. Indeed, the word *companions* comes from two Latin words: *com,* meaning "with," and *panis,* meaning "bread." Companions nourish our heart, mind, soul, and body. They are also the people with whom we can celebrate the sharing of bread.

Perhaps the most touching stories in the Bible are about companionship: the Last Supper, the wedding feast at Cana, the sharing of the loaves and the fishes, and Jesus' breaking of bread with the disciples on the road to Emmaus. Each incident of companionship with Jesus revealed more about his mercy, love, wisdom, suffering, and hope. When Jesus went to pray in the Garden of Olives, he craved the companionship of the Apostles. They let him down. But God sent the Spirit to inflame the hearts of the Apostles, and they became faithful companions to Jesus and to one another.

Throughout history other faithful companions have followed Jesus and the Apostles. These saints and mystics have also taken the journey from conversion, through suffering, to resurrection. Just as they were inspired by the holy people who went before them, so too may you be inspired by these saints and mystics and take them as your companions on your spiritual journey.

The Companions for the Journey series is a response to the spiritual hunger of Christians. This series makes available the rich spiritual teachings of mystics and guides whose wisdom can help us on our pilgrimage. As you complete the last meditation in each volume, it is hoped that you will feel supported, challenged, and affirmed by a soul-companion on your spiritual journey.

The spiritual hunger that has emerged over the years since the Second Vatican Council is a great sign of renewal in Christian life. People fill retreat programs and workshops on topics in spirituality. The demand for spiritual directors exceeds the number available. Interest in the lives and writings of saints and mystics is increasing as people search for models of whole and holy Christian life.

Praying with Pierre Teilhard de Chardin

Praying with Teilhard de Chardin is more than just a book about Pierre Teilhard de Chardin's spirituality. This book seeks to engage you in praying in the way that Teilhard did about issues and themes that were central to his experience. Each meditation can enlighten your understanding of his spirituality and lead you to reflect on your own experience.

The goal of *Praying with Teilhard de Chardin* is that you will discover Teilhard's rich spirituality and integrate his spirit and wisdom into your relationship with God, with your brothers and sisters, and with your own heart and mind.

Teilhard today is an attractive spiritual companion and guide in this created universe in which we live because of his biblically based perspective on the Christ of that universe. As a scientist of distinction, he brought the awe and wonder inherent in geology to where science, religion, and mystical spirituality come together in Christ.

Teilhard's Style of Prayer

Several styles of meditation are suitable for praying with Teilhard. In approaching Teilhard's thought and prayer, it may be useful to remember that he was so carried away by the cosmic grandeur of his vision that he burst out into conversation, or "colloquy"—a heart-to-heart talk with Jesus, the Holy Trinity, and with Mary, his mother. If you don't know where to start as you get acquainted with Jesus, pick up one of Teilhard's little books, such as *The Divine Milieu,* where you can read one of his colloquies slowly and prayerfully and make it your own if you wish. The words are not as important as the sincerity of the heart that utters its response to God's love. As you become more familiar with Teilhard's style of meditation, you may from time to time feel impelled to make up your own heartfelt response. Teilhard is an intellectual and many of his writings are a bit heady, but his spirituality is moving and attractive— it will go right to your heart because he is dealing with issues that most of us cherish deeply.

Suggestions for Praying with Teilhard

Get acquainted with Teilhard, your companion for this journey. You can do this by reading the introduction to this book, which begins on page 18. It consists of a brief biography organized so as to give some insight into various stages in Teilhard's spirituality and geological career through his own voluminous writings and writings about him. Because Teilhard placed so much emphasis spiritually on the importance of human achievement, and because scientists and engineers may often feel that they live in a world that is separated by a great wall from that of the churches, I want to underscore important milestones in his geological career to help bridge that gap. His great success as a writer on spirituality and on science and religion has unfortunately overshadowed his lifelong contributions as an accomplished and prolific geologist.

Create a sacred space. Find a sacred space that will provide you with an opportunity to become interiorly quiet or centered. This is important for scriptural meditations in which you use your imagination, your memory, or your several senses to make vivid and interesting the setting of a biblical passage. Your prayer is much less a history lesson than a story full of biblical imagery, seeing the persons, sensing what they are experiencing, smelling the dust, the animal smells in the village or countryside, the cool fragrance of shade from the hot sun, *and seeing yourself in the scene.* If the subject matter and setting of your prayer is engaging, distractions will be displaced by lively interest.

You may want to do some parts of these meditations outdoors, under the stars, in a chapel, or even in a busy city environment where you may have a sense of that vast network of busy people who make up the mystical Body of Christ. Even those things that you might have thought of as distractions in another environment should be used to help you "find God in all things." They may stimulate you to commune silently or to talk with God even in crowded public transportation.

One of my friends experiences his best prayer on the crowded and bustling train traveling roundtrip to work and home. Teilhard loved the quiet and seclusion of mountains, but he also loved the beehivelike activity of the city. Consciously and deliberately come to prayer with an open heart, joyful and optimistic because you are with your divine friend, Jesus, and your insightful companion, Teilhard. Determine ahead of time the length of the meditation period and stick with it.

Preview each meditation before beginning. As you scan the prayers, readings, and reflections, seize on whatever is personally most heartwarming or relevant to you. The goals are to develop a meaningful relationship with Jesus and to movitate you. Remember that you are on an exciting journey, so focus on those aspects of the scenery that will make your trip through life most memorable.

Read slowly, meditatively, and with relish. Be patient with yourself, remembering that no fixed amount of material must be covered in your meditation period; each meditation is a smorgasbord. Your prayer is intended to enrich your life. Remember that while we may think, "I'm too busy to pray or to worship," none of us can afford not to pray, especially the liturgical prayers of the church by which God takes us in hand, as William J. Leonard so beautifully says:

> God's shaping hands are the fashioning liturgy of the Church, by which, to be sure, we worship him, but by which, also, he molds us to the likeness of his Son, the

archetype of our holiness. Baptism, Confirmation, Orders, Marriage are not simply milestones, . . . they are . . . the beginnings of a new intimacy of God with his material, during which he labors unremittingly to achieve in us the expression of his thought. (P. 189)

Use the reflections. Teilhard's writings and thought commonly are poetic and filled with symbolism that enriched his life. The same is true of the Scriptures. Both have the potential to nourish and inspire us just as poetry and great books do because they humanize us. The theory of Jesuit education has been summed up by the Boston College theologian Michael Himes, "Whatever humanizes, divinizes" (p. 24). As we learn to pattern our humanity more authentically on that of Jesus, we share more fully in his divinity (as Paul says in Philippians 2:5–7).

The reflections are meant as possible helps in looking back at your experience in the other parts of the meditation preparation and prayer itself. A key question to reflect on is, "Was the prayer activity more like something that went on in my head alone, or was it something that nourished my heart, made me feel loved, energized and that connected me in a constructive way with those who are important in my life?" The key question to ask yourself is, "Has this prayer period nourished me in pursuit of my passion?" If your answer is yes, you have had a good prayer experience. When Jesus came down from the mountain after praying, he was energized so as to pursue what he felt passionate about.

Write in a journal. Writing an account of what you did in meditation and, perhaps more importantly, what happened to you in your heart in the prayer period is an important part of the journey. Write your reaction to questions such as, "What do you react to positively or negatively in Teilhard's life and words, and in the biblical passages?" An honest response will help you to understand whether and to what extent Jesus and you, as well as Teilhard and you, are on the same path at all. Write honestly about where you are, or might like to be, emotionally and spiritually.

In writing in your journal, write regularly, keep it short, and review it from time to time. If you start off writing a lot, you are likely to quickly give it up. Write just enough so that when you read your journal reflection, you can remember what your heart was saying to you. Keep it short enough so that you will have the time and energy to write in your journal regularly, preferably daily. Note how Teilhard was always writing!

Reflect on what you have written from time to time, say once a week. That will allow you to see beneficial changes that may be going on in you, new perspectives, new growth patterns. Over a period of time, reflection on your journal entries will reveal new pathways that have become enlivening for you. A question that may be significant is, "In what ways am I becoming more alive, more caring, more grateful for the gifts that have come into my life?"

Use awareness meditation. The following prayer is a prayerful way to discover God's presence in daily life. It is a prayer based on gratitude for the past and the present and on hope for the future.

1. Prayer for insight: I take a moment to become interiorly quiet, or centered, by focusing my gaze and attention, and by relaxed regular breathing. I pray somewhat as follows, "Holy Spirit give me insight, an increased awareness of your divine presence, so as to recognize your divinity in the persons and events of my day."

2. Prayer for gratitude: Give me a spirit of gratitude, for being—for being here—and especially for sharing in the divine life of the Trinity, for the Eucharist, for family, friends, and for all of life's gifts. May I deepen my attitude of gratitude by thanking you, God, for the special gift of mystery that ornaments, but may easily hide, if I am not reflective, the deeper meaning of events and persons in my life.

3. Daily discovery of God: Holy Spirit, give me the insight to detect your divine Presence as I slowly review the past day, letting the parade of events move over the screen of my mind as I relax in your presence. I am listening attentively to you, Lord, so that you may show me where you are meeting me, challenging me, and subtly revealing your caring presence and love.

I review my attitudes and actions in light of Christ's, focusing on feelings of fear, anger, pain, turmoil, anxiety, joy, love, exultation, courage, and so on. I try to discover why my attitudes draw me toward God or toward self, why they are like or unlike Christ's.

I pray, "Christ, my friend, grant that by this awareness I may discover where you were present but where I did not recognize you. Reveal to me the part of my life, especially the area of greatest weakness, in which you, Lord, are drawing me to a deeper conversion."

4. *God's desire for my love:* As I grow in realization of Jesus' awesome desire for my love, contrition and sorrow for my failure to respond to the Lord may well up in my heart. Inspire me, my Savior, to respond to love with love, and to pray for forgiveness. Inspired by the Spirit, may I love the Lord, my God, with my whole heart, my whole mind, and all my strength.

5. *Prayer for strength and guidance:* Hopeful resolve for the day coming over the horizon is a discernment activity in which I honestly examine and evaluate my hope or discouragement in looking to the future. Lord, give me insight to become aware, even if sometimes painfully, of specific ways in which you are revealing yourself to me, as you did to your friends on the road to Emmaus. With Saint Paul I pray with confidence, I leave the past behind and with hands outstretched to whatever lies ahead, I go straight for the goal.

(This awareness meditation is based on Skehan, p. 12, and is modeled on a kind of prayer that Ignatius of Loyola, founder of the Society of Jesus, recommended for every day.)

Take action. Highly appropriate activities for praying with Teilhard are to walk and sit in nature, depending on what is available. If you are at the seashore or looking at a beautiful landscape, you will need no further instructions— you are already in a part of the universe conducive to communing with God.

Using the Meditations for Group Prayer

The meditations in this book have been used successfully in a variety of ways with groups enrolled in Teilhardian Spirituality in Everyday Life Retreats sponsored initially by the Jesuit community of Boston College and the Faith and Science Exchange, originally founded by Rev. Barbara Smith-Moran, SOSc, and the Episcopal Diocese of Massachusetts. Each meditation contains such a large amount of diverse material that it would probably create overload to attempt group meditation covering everything. I suggest that each meditation may be suitable for several personal prayer periods in the course of a week preparatory to the group meeting. If the group meets weekly, then the entire meditation may be addressed in the meeting. It is important that the group become centered, or focused, by a short period of quiet preparation for prayer. I follow the practice used in the Buddhist monastery of striking my meditation bell, which has the effect of helping the group to settle into a divine milieu.

A possible format for group prayer is for the leader or one of the participants to read slowly the "About Teilhard" section followed by a selection from "Teilhard's Words" or from "God's Word" for silent meditation. This can fruitfully be followed by some ideas contained in the "Reflection" section, or preferably, by thoughts or feelings evoked by the prayer itself. It is important for members of the group to reach a point where they can share what is most meaningful from their personal perspective. In the sharing period, it is important to evoke personal implications of religious or personal spirituality rather than information as King has emphasized (*The Spirit of One Earth*, p. 28).

The best advice I can give is to trust the Spirit to lead the group and don't concentrate too much on the structure as such.

A format that has proved successful in our Teilhardian Spirituality in Everyday Life Retreats is also presented in the book *Soul at Work: Reflections on a Spirituality of Working*, by Rev. Barbara Smith-Moran, SOSc. This volume has been enthusiastically received by the large number of staff members and their spiritual companions of Boston College who have engaged in short retreats under the direction of Walter Conlan, SJ, consultant for Ignatian spirituality in the department of human resources of Boston College.

✧ Preface ✧

Teilhard de Chardin's perspective is so exciting to so many because he was personally aware that human beings have a deep-seated longing for their life to be significant and for their work to have permanent value. But Christians had that assurance even before Teilhard; Jesus told his followers so but in different words. However, Teilhard's perspective on the cosmic implications of Christ's Incarnation, based on his understanding of passages of Saint Paul, has imparted a new appreciation of the awesome personal value and permanence of all that we do and are. In times past the link between the created world and spirituality was commonly lacking; this bonding that we feel between the Earth and ourselves as well as having the motivation to participate vigorously in the mainstream human work of "building the Earth" has been reaffirmed gloriously by Teilhard.

As a youngster growing up in Houlton, Maine, I often wished that I had a friend who would be so compatible that he would want to do all the things that I wanted to do, and would want to share my most intimate thoughts, emotions, and desires. In many ways that was fanciful because I had brothers and sisters whom I loved and were close to me but who as individuals themselves, quite rightly, would not always share all of my interests. But still I had longings for even deeper friendship. I have come to realize the importance of such dreams because that longing for an alter ego, or another self, expresses a kind of desire or cosmic sense that is a longing for the infinite, a longing that can be fully realized only in an intimate friendship with Jesus of Nazareth and to an important level with Teilhard, our companion for the journey.

I am grateful to Rev. Barbara Smith-Moran, SOSc, Donald J. Plocke, SJ, and Gail Bucher, who have participated as directors of the Teilhardian Spirituality in Everyday Life Retreats over the past eight years. Smith-Moran's book *Soul at Work* consists of materials developed during the first few years of our collaboration in directing these retreats and that were enthusiastically received as retreat materials in book form. I am grateful to Thomas M. King, SJ, Georgetown University, and James F. Salmon, SJ, Loyola College of Baltimore, for helping to immerse me in Teilhardian spirituality during an eight-day retreat in the 1980s at the Jesuit Center for Spiritual Growth, Wernersville, Maryland, and for sessions that they and Prof. Frank McGuire organized for studies of Teilhard's thought and spirituality at selected annual conference meetings of Cosmos and Creation at Loyola College of Baltimore.

I am grateful to Prof. John E. Ebel, director of Weston Observatory, department of geology and geophysics, Boston College, for support during this research. I express my gratitude to Patricia C. Tassia and to Tracy S. Downing, of the Weston Observatory staff, and Patricia Rose Pflaumer, who, in proofreading, have materially improved the final product. I am indebted to former "Teilhardians" who have let me understand how Teilhard's spirituality has nourished them. In particular I have been inspired additionally by Sarah Appleton-Weber, Karl and Nicole Schmitz-Moormann, Ursula King, and Harvey D. Egan, SJ, through their scholarly works and in stimulating personal contacts.

✧ Introduction ✧

Pierre Teilhard de Chardin: A Companion

Pierre Teilhard de Chardin (TAY-ar-deh-shar-dan), a Jesuit priest and professional geologist, has become, at first glance, an unexpected, if not an unlikely, hero and inspiration for many people who value spirituality or learning, or both. As a stretcher bearer–priest in a Moroccan regiment during all of World War I, he was admired and beloved by Christians and Muslims alike. As a geologist in the field on expeditions into the deserts and mountains of Asia, he was well received by his fellow scientists as well as by camel drivers and desert people along the way.

Teilhard was an attractive companion to most of those with whom he came in contact because of his optimistic outlook on life. He recognized that Yahweh, the Lord of the Hebrew Bible and the God of the New Testament, really and truly shepherds the flock. He lived with the confidence that the God who in the Book of Genesis saw that creation was good, in the end, would return the orientation of the chaotic and sinful world to God and God's purposes in the New Jerusalem as is foretold in the Book of Revelation, chapters 21–22.

Pierre Teilhard de Chardin is best known by part of his family name, Teilhard. Although he has wide name recognition, relatively few people seem to have thoroughly read many of his voluminous writings. English translations of these are now widely available, as well as commentaries and unpublished letters on the broad spectrum of his thought and spirituality.

Teilhard, it seems, has been the beneficiary of good press generated by biographers who include theologians, philoso-

18

phers, and scientists. But he has also been criticized for his efforts in, and methods for, bridging the gap between science and religion. Nevertheless, I, as a Christian, who is also a Jesuit priest and professional geologist, have discovered in Teilhard a most stimulating companion for my spiritual journey. In these pages I endeavor to point out some of the influences on Teilhard and his thought and spirituality as he evolved throughout a long and adventuresome lifetime. Such influences included Teilhard's family and his numerous friends. He was an avid reader and an equally prolific author, letter writer, and conversationalist.

Teilhard's many manuscripts and essays, consisting of over five hundred items, were first published chiefly in French or remained unpublished before his death in 1955. Even after his writings were published in English in the late 1950s and early 1960s, it took a long time for them to be widely accepted by theologians and philosophers because Teilhard's thought was expressed, in part at least, in terms that he invented. Because many of his expressions were unconventional, it took many scholars, theologians, and biographers years of examining his thought and writings before coming to a sympathetic appreciation of them. A noted French theologian, Henri de Lubac, SJ, came to Teilhard's defense during Vatican Council II and in books early on. It is undoubtedly because of his analysis of Teilhard's writings, and his stature as a theologian who would later be elevated to the rank of cardinal, that the cloud of suspicion over Teilhard was lifted. In the process a substantial number of Teilhard's ideas that he based on biblical texts of Saints Paul and John have found their way into discussions of, and in some instances were ultimately incorporated into, documents of the Second Vatican Council.

Over the approximate one-half century since Teilhard's death, Teilhard's writings have been recognized as very exciting Christocentric extensions and interpretations of traditional Catholic teaching. For our purposes in this volume, it is enough to emphasize those events in Teilhard's life and his perspectives that may nourish our spirituality, as well as to provide to the extent possible, brief descriptions of how he came to develop these ideas.

Formative Childhood Influences

Teilhard's mother and father fashioned an environment that stimulated and nurtured profoundly both his religious and natural history interests. He was born in 1881, the fourth of eleven children. His father, Emmanuel, was a country gentleman who had a number of hobbies and intellectual interests, including maps and natural science. In pursuit of natural science in the field, he and his family members assembled substantial collections of birds, insects, plants, and of course, rocks. He also belonged to an ancient and noble line of the Auvergne region in central France. His mother, Berthe-Adèle de Dompierre d'Hermoy, was a noblewoman from Picardy, in northern France. Both father and mother were devout Catholics, whose dominant influences respectively seem to have been expressed in Teilhard's double-barreled preoccupation with science and religion.

His father was a forceful man, highly regarded in the region, who devoted himself to the education of his children and demanded of them full participation in a disciplined family life. Teilhard's childhood photographs suggest an intense, highly motivated youngster. He said that he owed many things to his father, but especially "certain well-defined ambitions, no doubt, but even more a certain basic balance on which everything else was built" (*Divine Milieu*, p. 17). His reputation throughout his life as an indefatigable geologist in the field and laboratory may possibly be traced to well-disciplined habits formed early in life. As a boy Teilhard apparently had a somewhat reclusive temperament; but as an adult who seemed to enjoy every opportunity to share ideas and to make new friends and meet new colleagues, he possessed a quietly self-assured personality.

Search for the Most Durable

Even in his early years, Teilhard, in taking advantage of the opportunities offered to, and perhaps even demanded of, him by his father, was unwittingly preparing himself to think the "great thoughts" for which he became so well known. He was naturally drawn to introspection that focused on searching for the most durable and lasting material as a sort of anchor for his life. That quest led him to fix on iron as the hardest and most incorruptible object until, to his disappointment, he discovered that iron rusted. Then he fixed his anchor on quartzite, a hard and durable rock. He must have been a precocious child because he noted in *The Heart of Matter* that his earliest childhood memories were of his dominant passion for the Absolute. Although as he matured he came to recognize that spirit was more durable than iron or quartzite, which for a time was his Absolute. "The truth is," he said "that even at the peak of my spiritual trajectory, I was never to feel at home unless immersed in an Ocean of Matter" (King, *Spirit of Fire*, p. 7). As a mature scholar working with human remains preserved in stratified rock, Teilhard, whose preoccupation was with humankind's place in nature, must have felt right at home. With volcanic ash and lava cones forming the foothills of the Puy de Dome country of Auvergne in the distance in his own backyard, how could he have failed to direct his curiosity to geology? Near his own birthplace was born his strong "cosmic sense," which later was supplemented by a similarly sturdy "human sense" and "Christic sense." In his intensive search for what was most durable in the world, Teilhard found his way to geology by his passionate study of the science of rocks.

In spring and summer, the family occupied an ample sprawling farmhouse by a river in Sarcenat and Murol and at certain times gathered with their cousins, the Teillard-Chambon branch of the family in the townhouse in Clermont-Ferrand. During childhood days Teilhard established a relationship with Marguerite-Marie Teillard-Chambon that later in life resulted in voluminous and significant correspondence chronicled in his books *Writings in Time of War* and *The Making of a Mind*, largely compiled and edited by her while he served in the French army. We companions of Teilhard owe much to his cousin Marguerite for having preserved not only his essays but also his correspondence with her. These volumes record many of Teilhard's ideas and thought at this early and most significant period in his life. The bond of deep friendship and understanding between

Teilhard and Marguerite was strong and long-lasting. As a scholarly person, she was an active participant in discussions and conversations with Teilhard; as a deeply religious person, she looked to Teilhard for spiritual direction.

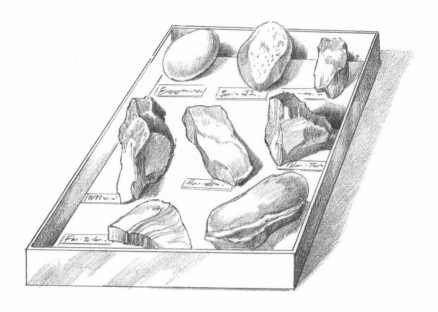

The Jesuit Boarding School

Just before he turned eleven, Teilhard went off to the École Libre de Notre-Dame de Mongrè, a few miles north of Lyons. This Jesuit school was a leading institution for education in the natural sciences in an environment of Spartan discipline, where learning and devotion were jointly fostered. Teilhard has been described as "an exemplary, though rather taciturn, and even self-absorbed pupil" (King, *Spirit of Fire*, p. 10) whose name appeared several times on plaques in the school corridor as having received a first prize. One of his teachers described young Teilhard:

> Thirty years ago I had a little third-year pupil from Auvergne, very intelligent, first in every subject, but discon-

certingly sophisticated. Even the most restive or dull-witted boys sometimes took a real interest in their work. . . . Not so this boy: and it was only long afterwards that I learnt the secret of his seeming indifference. Transporting his mind far away from us was another, a jealous and absorbing passion—rocks.

We know a good deal about his religious life. After making his first communion on Ascension Day 1892, he was admitted to the Sodality [a sodality is one of the religious societies typical of Jesuit schools for extracurricular participation by students to help provide inspiration, motivation, and guidance] of St. Aloysius Gonzaga, and later (1895) to that of the Immaculate Conception, making his act of consecration to Our Lady on the feast of the Immaculate Conception. (Cuenot, pp. 4–5)

Throughout his life Our Lady held a special place in his spirituality; Mary was to become the central figure in Teilhard's understanding of the "Eternal Feminine."

Teilhard as a Jesuit in Training

In 1899, Teilhard's first year in the Jesuit novitiate at Aix-en-Provence, Pope Leo XIII consecrated the whole of humanity to the Sacred Heart, a devotion symbolized by fire of love, a central image in Teilhard's writings and thought. Following his first vows on 25 March 1901, he began a program of collegiate studies in literature leading to his first degree, at the University of Caen. That same year the French government passed laws constraining the activities of religious orders, so Teilhard, and other Jesuits, fled to the Isle of Jersey for his next four years of collegiate studies.

Scientific Studies in Jersey

In Jersey, Teilhard was immersed in philosophy, theology, and the sciences until 1905. Captivated by the bedrock on the island's shores, he devoted his holidays to a study of its geology.

He obviously took great delight in geological fieldwork as such, but in addition,

> his inner attraction to the great forces of nature, so deeply rooted in earlier childhood experiences, became so immensely strong that it awakened in him a vibrant cosmic consciousness. . . . But when surrendering himself "to the embrace of the visible and tangible universe," he learned to feel the hand of God. And then he saw, "as though in ecstasy, that *through all of nature I was immersed in God*. (King, *Spirit of Fire*, p. 19)

Teaching and Fieldwork in Egypt

In September 1905, Teilhard was sent to Collège de la Sainte Famille in Cairo to teach physics and chemistry and to serve as curator of the museum. He summed up his three-year experience of teaching and a modest program of regular scientific fieldwork: "I . . . experienced such sense of wonder in Egypt" (p. 24). That his study of fossil sea life was significant is indicated by one of the fossils that he discovered being named *Teilhardi* by the Geological Society of France. Teilhard's experience of the great beauty of the Egyptian desert, its immensity and its silence, reverberated in his soul for years:

> Most important was an eight days' excursion in early April 1907 to the desert area of El Faiyum, southwest of Cairo, on which he wrote an article soon afterward. . . . This first real expedition left an indelible impression on Teilhard's mind. . . . His cosmic sense, his sense of the All, so vividly experienced since childhood and youth, certainly vastly expanded and grew through his prolonged stay in Egypt. (Pp. 27–28)

> The East flowed over me in a first wave of exoticism. I gazed at it and drank it in eagerly—the country itself . . . its light, its vegetation, its fauna, its deserts. (Mortier and Auboux, p. 36)

A letter from Teilhard to a friend gives a glimpse into his pursuits at this time:

Here are my latest finds. M. Priem has talked at the Geological Society of France about my fishes' teeth from
Mount Mokattam and on the jawbone of the Sirenian. At
New Year I spent a week in Upper Egypt and I brought
back from the Minya deposits a store of echinids which
are the delight of M. Fourtau. He is writing an article
about them . . . these results show what one can do in
between classroom duties . . . if you take the trouble to
find a companion who doesn't mind . . . turning over
stones . . . in the desert, or detaching some big fossil
from a rocky wall, in heat like a furnace. (P. 35)

Impressions from his desert expeditions were far-reaching because they

contributed to an increasing awareness of the immensity
of matter and the grandeur of Christ. . . . This dialogue
with the East, more specifically with India and China, was
to continue during the whole of Teilhard's life. It can never be sufficiently emphasized that however often the
dress of the explorer disguised the priest Teilhard was of
the blood and temper of the great Jesuit missionaries.
(Cuenot, p. 10)

Theology Studies and Ordination

In 1908, Teilhard was called back to Hastings, on the Sussex
coast of England, to begin four years of theological studies. He
was ordained to the priesthood on 24 August 1911 in the presence of his mother and father, who received communion from
his newly anointed hands. After completing a fourth and final
year of theological studies, Teilhard returned to Paris, where
in July 1912 he was interviewed by the famous geologist
Marcelin Boule, a brilliant specialist in comparative paleontology. This meeting launched him "into what has been my
whole life ever since: research and adventure in the field of
paleontology" (King, *Spirit of Fire*, p. 41).

In 1913, a British scientist described new fossil plants in
the *Journal of the Geological Society of London*. Because these
were forms that Teilhard had discovered in Hastings, one was
given the genus name *Teilhardia* and a species, *Teilhardi*.

World War I Stretcher Bearer

As Europe was plunging into World War I, Teilhard's tertian-ship, that is, the final year of a Jesuit's training, was begun at Canterbury. In December 1914 Teilhard joined the French army as a medical orderly; before long, at his own request, he was sent as a stretcher bearer to the front ranks. Priests in France were required to serve in the military, so Teilhard chose to be an ordinary soldier rather than to enjoy the privileges of higher rank. His regiment of Zouaves and the Moroccan Tirailleurs participated in the main battles of the war. He personally faced death almost daily but served the troops with complete dedication, giving rise to his great popularity. The soldiers came to rely on him and drew courage and strength of purpose from his dedication and faith. Teilhard not only exercised great leadership but came through these major battles completely unscathed. In addition to receiving several war decorations, he was made Chevalier de la Légion d'Honneur at the request of his former regiment, the Moroccan Tirailleurs.

The tertianship consists of an intensive, secluded thirty-day retreat, and other experiences in ascetical and pastoral theology in preparation for solemn final vows. For Teilhard his war service became his tertianship and preparation for final vows; his essay "The Priest" was written on this occasion, and is an early draft of his classic meditation "The Mass on the World."

Between 1916 and 1919, Teilhard authored eighteen essays amid the horrors of war at the front, which he sent to his cousin Marguerite but did not intend most of them for publication. His constant prayer while working in the trenches was "The Priest." Later in the field in Asia he composed a quite different version, "The Mass on the World." These were published eventually as *Writings in Time of War* (1965). François Mauriac praised the essays in these words: "The most optimistic view a Christian thinker has ever held of this criminal world was conceived at Verdun" (King, *Spirit of Fire,* p. 66).

In Paris After the War

In Paris Teilhard was appointed to the chair of geology at the Institut Catholique, left vacant by the death of Professor Boussac, a position in which he would inevitably rise to the upper echelons in French academic circles. This was a time, however, in which any who dared to speak on religious topics were bound to be closely scrutinized by the watchdogs of Catholic orthodoxy. Having survived religious persecution at the hands of anticlericals when they fled to Jersey two decades earlier, men like Teilhard were inevitably going to suffer even more from the teeth of rabid, misguided watchdogs of "orthodoxy."

> It was a critical moment; and Valensin [a friend and mentor of Teilhard], knowing the almost naïve abandon with which Teilhard behaved characteristically, as well as the unfriendly eyes that watched out for those who might be thought of as speaking for the Church, could only stand despairingly aside and watch. (Lukas and Lukas, p. 68)

They did not have a long wait! It seems that divine providence had endowed Teilhard with a combination of a brilliant, razor-sharp intellect and a heart attracted to both the natural history of the Earth and to a creative spirituality that became a glorious superstructure on traditional Christianity. This combination yoked to his prodigious energy and a blissful naïveté with regard to ecclesiastical sensibilities made everyone in church circles nervous except Teilhard.

Teilhard was acutely aware of and concerned with a religious crisis that brought traditional understanding of God into conflict with new perspectives on the natural world. After World War I, he recognized in the growing attraction of Buddhism and other forms of spirituality the need for new ways of expressing worship and adoration: "Since the war he had realized that humankind formed a single whole, a large, cosmic reality that far transcended individuals and groups. This human reality . . . was like a dynamic, living organism . . . , a network whose threads stretched over the face of the whole earth" (King, *Spirit of Fire*, p. 87).

For a time Teilhard called the thinking Earth the anthroposphere, but in 1925 devised a new name, the noosphere.

This was to become one of his key ideas, an absolutely central element of his vision. Just as the zone of life—the total mass of living organisms—was the biosphere, a living layer above the non-living world of the geosphere, so there was yet another, thinking layer, a sphere of mind and spirit surrounding the globe. It is like a thinking envelope of the earth of which all humans are part. All contribute to it through their thinking, feeling, connecting, and interacting with each other, and above all through their powers of love. The emergence of the noosphere is an important step forward in becoming human, in the process of transformation he called "hominization." (P. 88)

First Expeditions in China

In 1923 Teilhard was sent by the Paris Museum to participate in a scientific expedition along the Yellow River in China. That four-month expedition was so fruitful that Teilhard extended his stay so that he could make another expedition to the high Mongolian plateau and the Gobi Desert in 1924. Between expeditions he visited Peking, where he met American anthropologists, paleontologists, and geologists, and scientists from many other countries. A new world was opening for Teilhard because he now saw geology in a much broader perspective and correctly forecast the directions in which the science would develop in succeeding decades. Although Teilhard was aware of theories of continental drift, data critical for developing theories of large-scale plate tectonic movements of the Earth's crust were yet to be discovered, in large part due to the kinds of research that Teilhard envisioned.

The expeditions that Teilhard made in China and his contacts with Chinese colleagues and other foreign nationals working in China expanded his geological and paleontological horizons. Eastern Asia had become attractive for the significant research opportunities that it appeared to offer. His enthusiastic reception at the Institut Catholique and the Paris Museum and his recognition as a rising star by a wide circle of scientific colleagues made it attractive for him to keep one foot in France and one in China for the next quarter of a century.

The decades between his first expeditions in China and his departure in 1946 were scientifically Teilhard's most fruitful period. He received a number of significant honors, such as the Mendel Medal awarded by the Augustinian Fathers of Villanova University in 1937 and induction into the Academy of Sciences of France, signs of a growing recognition that he was nearing the highest level of academic achievement. In addition he made time to write on science and religion and especially to rethink and expand on ideas and themes that he had explored earlier in his career.

Exile in China

One of his papers was on original sin. By 1925 it had landed him in deep trouble.

> A bloc of conservative French bishops [was] so disturbed by Teilhard's influence that they complained to the Holy Office, which, in turn, put pressure on the Jesuits. . . .
>
> It had never required much to make the Jesuit general, Vladimir Ledochowski, take action against a troublesome subordinate. . . .
>
> . . . Teilhard, he ordered, was to . . . leave his post at the Institut Catholique, and . . . betake himself from France.
>
> . . . To top it off, Ledochowski sent his spiritual son a personal letter, reminding him how much "useless work" the simple possession of the "Deposit of Faith" spared the Catholic intellectual. . . . On April 5, 1926, Teilhard boarded the steamship *Ankor* for the Far East—now, in every sense, an exile, uncertain as to whether he would ever see his native land again. (Lukas and Lukas, pp. 91–95)

You Can't Keep a Good Man Down

As Teilhard traveled back to China in June 1926, he settled down to writing *The Divine Milieu*—"the sort of ascetical or mystical teaching that I have been living and preaching so long" (*Letters from a Traveller*, p. 133). On his return journey to China, his spirit began to be uplifted as he traveled the vast spaces, and so he began to "dream of writing 'the book of the Earth' which would resonate with 'the note of the All,' a book for people like Ida Treat who were far removed from the Christian faith" (King, *Spirit of Fire*, p. 112) and to whom he wrote as follows in October 1926:

> The only book I want to and need to write would not be the book of China, but "the book of the Earth." In short, I would like to speak as I think, without concern for what is accepted, with the sole idea of translating as faithfully as possible what I hear murmuring in me like a voice or a song which are not of me, but of the World in me. (*Letters to Two Friends*, 1926–1952, p. 44)

By February 1927 Teilhard was invited by the Carnegie Foundation to supervise research on vertebrate and human fossils in China, a position that expanded his resources and responsibilities, while still remaining as the Paris Museum representative. He writes about this time in *Letters from a Traveller*:

> I now find myself (with several colleagues of course) in charge of geological work in China. In my own special field my concern is now to clear up some geological formations over an area as large as half Europe.
> . . . My most active moments are still when I am saying my "Mass upon the altar of the world" to divinise the new day. (Pp. 137–140).

Years of Crowning Achievement

Teilhard's exile from France and his return to China were but the beginning of a twenty-one year period of unparalleled scholarly productivity in geology and paleontology on three continents in association with some of the leading scientists in the project countries. Teilhard's work was principally concerned at first with China and then with neighboring countries, a vast area of eastern and central Asia. Later, important scientific interests required him to travel to Java, in connection with the discovery of the Java man, and to South Africa. In 1929 Teilhard was appointed adviser to the Geological Survey of China.

Because Teilhard was meticulous about regional correlations, he became progressively more involved in geology in the service of paleontology in general and human paleontology in particular, as is indicated by George Barbour's comments about the spectacular Chou-Kou-Tien deposit, in which the skull of Peking man was found in 1929:

> As study of the fossils progressed, it became clear that the relatively isolated position of Chou-Kou-Tien—thousands of miles from the nearest localities where other Late Cenozoic strata were known (Japan, Java, India, etc.)—ruled out any simple faunal correlations as a means of setting an exact age to the Peking man "horizon." [Teilhard's colleague] Davidson Black realized that the Cenozoic Laboratory could attain its objectives only by extending its reconnaissances right across China and into Central Asia. . . .
>
> Black had already made contact with authorities in India and the Middle East, as a first step in his plan to lead a Cenozoic Expedition into the mid-continent. He came to New York with Teilhard and Grabau in the summer of 1933, just before the Washington meeting of the XVIII International Geological Congress, with a view to securing from the Rockefeller Foundation approval for this project. (Barbour, p. 60)

Because Teilhard's writings on spirituality have been so enthusiastically received over the years, particularly since their publication after his death in 1955, he is much better known in North America for these than for his geological research. As a result Teilhard's scientific accomplishments may have been assumed incorrectly to have been relatively insignificant. That Teilhard was a world-class geologist and paleontologist, however, is attested to by George Barbour, himself a distinguished American geologist working in China at the time. Dr. Barbour worked closely with Teilhard on a number of projects for a quarter of a century. He describes expeditions in which they both participated in his delightful book *In the Field with Teilhard de Chardin*. It provides a significant perspective on Teilhard as a geologist, a man, and a conversationalist—someone who engaged Barbour in discussions of his current religio-scientific ideas around the campfire toward the end of a day of fieldwork. Teilhard inscribed his important religious work *How I Believe* "to my other self, George B. Barbour."

In 1929, after the discovery of teeth of the Peking man, Davidson Black, a Canadian scientist, organized the Cenozoic Laboratory as a joint research center in the Geological Survey of China, supported by the Rockefeller Foundation. Teilhard worked in the Cenozoic Laboratory in Peking and at the Chou-Kou-Tien site, where he was in charge of identifying the fossils. Black, one of Teilhard's closest colleagues and dearest friends, died suddenly in 1934, and Teilhard was appointed acting director. Teilhard spent a part of 1935–1936 first in India in the Siwalik Hills with the Yale-Cambridge research team under Helmut de Terra, explorer and geographer, and later in Burma with the Harvard-Carnegie expedition led by Hallam Movius. (Teilhard visited Movius at Harvard University in about 1949 while I was a graduate student in geology there.)

Although it could hardly be claimed that Teilhard was a consummate diplomat where the papacy and his writings are concerned, he was a true bridge builder in scientific circles. He was the one that scientists turned to when disputes arose, as happened on the Citroën expedition across Asia.

The Citroën expedition was initiated by the French automobile firm Citroën, which chose Teilhard as the official geologist for its trans-Asian expedition. The firm wanted to test its vehicles under extreme conditions. As one of forty scientists and engineers, Teilhard set out in May 1931 from Peking to cross the Gobi Desert. This was his most rewarding expedition, due to ten months of tireless research under unbelievably adverse conditions.

After the Japanese invaded north China in 1940, Teilhard's ability to carry on fieldwork was tightly restricted, so he and Pierre Leroy, SJ, organized the Geobiological Institute in the Legation Quarter of Peking, salvaging what collections they could from the Cenozoic Laboratory and the Tientsin Museum. The volume *The Future of Man*, is a collection of essays concerned with the future, assembled after Teilhard died.

The book for which Teilhard is best known is *The Phenomenon of Man* (1959), translated by Bernard Wall, and more recently *The Human Phenomenon* (1999), translated and edited by Sarah Appleton-Weber. Teilhard wrote his first essay on *Le phénomène humain* in 1928 in Paris.

Teilhard states that to be properly understood, *The Human Phenomenon* must be read "exclusively as a scientific study" of the phenomenon, the "*whole* of the phenomenon," and not as "an *explanation* of the world" (Appleton-Weber, p. 1). His position is that the sciences have been so compartmentalized as to prevent a complete study of the human being as well as a complete understanding of the human beings' place in nature.

> For Teilhard the development of humankind is not an anomalous element of the universe, but it is "a fundamental phenomenon—*the* supreme phenomenon of nature: that in which, in a unique complexity of material and moral factors, one of the principal acts of universal evolution is not only experienced but lived by us." (King, *Spirit of Fire*, p. 121)

In *Spirit of Fire*, King quotes Teilhard further:

> "There is a science of the universe without man. There is also a science of man as marginal to the universe; but there is not yet a science of the universe that embraces man as such. Present-day physics . . . does not yet give a place to thought, which means that it still exists in complete independence of the most remarkable phenomenon exposed by nature to our observation." (P. 121)

Teilhard's Last Years

In 1947 Teilhard was preparing with George Barbour to participate in the University of California's expedition to South Africa when he suffered a heart attack. It was four years later that he realized his desire to complete that excursion, this time as a research associate of the New York–based Wenner-Gren Foundation for Anthropological Research. By that time Wenner-Gren had furnished office facilities in its New York headquarters, where Teilhard worked during the remaining years of his life.

A month before his death, Teilhard wrote:

The joy and strength of my life will have lain in the realisation that when the two ingredients—God and the world—were brought together they set up an endless mutual reaction, producing a blaze of such intense brilliance that all of the depths of the world were lit up for me. (*Divine Milieu*, p. 37)

On the morning of 10 April 1955, Teilhard, after saying a private Mass, went to high Mass at Saint Patrick's Cathedral in Manhattan. He then met Rhoda de Terra and her daughter to attend a concert, after which he had tea at their apartment. There he was stricken by a massive heart attack. He had made his confession the previous day to a fellow Jesuit, and right after his heart attack, the sacrament of Anointing was administered by Fr. Martin Geraghty, a Jesuit from nearby Saint Ignatius Church. Teilhard was buried in the cemetery of what is now the former Jesuit novitiate on the Hudson River at Poughkeepsie, now on the property of the Culinary Institute of America. Access to Teilhard's grave may be had by his "praying companions on the journey" by permission at the reception desk of the institute.

On that beautiful Easter Sunday in April 1955, Teilhard, celebrating the joy of the Resurrection, the promise of his own rising to everlasting life, went to possess the Christ whom he had long envisioned in the blaze of victory.

Lord, since with every instinct of my being and through all the changing fortunes of my life, it is you whom I have ever sought, you whom I have set at the heart of universal matter, it will be in a resplendence which shines through all things and in which all things are ablaze, that I shall have the felicity of closing my eyes. (P. 42)

Jesus, the Heart of My Vision

Theme: God created men and women so that they might seek and find the God who, in Teilhard's words, is "as pervasive and perceptible as the atmosphere in which we are bathed" (*Divine Milieu*, p. 46).

Opening prayer: Lord Jesus, you touched the eyes of "the man born blind," healed him and gave him sight. Touch the eyes of my heart and mind.

About Teilhard

As a geologist studying the fossil remains of primates and early man in the second and later decades of the twentieth century, Teilhard saw evidence of biological evolution at every turn. His insights into the letters of Paul and the Gospel of John led him to see that the Kingdom of Christ is also undergoing an evolution. That as-yet-unfinished work of the Kingdom is an evolution in the sense that Jesus, the head of creation, provides each of us members of the Body of Christ in our own time and place with opportunities to collaborate with him in building the Earth as cocreators and coredeemers.

In writing *The Phenomenon of Man* as a bridge from science to religion, Teilhard developed the concept of a universe evolving, being attracted along converging lines of energy toward its final goal, Christ, the head of the universe. As a kind of neutral scientific term in discussions with non-Christians, Teilhard used the term *Omega,* the last letter of the Greek alphabet, for that end point, which is Christ.

Pause: Ask yourself, "How attuned am I to seeing or recognizing God in the events of my life?"

Teilhard's Words

Seeing. We might say the whole of life lies in that verb—if not ultimately, at least essentially. Fuller being in closer union; such is the kernel and conclusion of this book. But let us emphasize the point: union increases only through an increase in consciousness, that is to say in vision. And that, doubtless, is why the history of the living world can be summarized as the elaboration of ever more perfect eyes within a cosmos in which there is always more to be seen. . . . To try to see more and better is not a matter of whim or curiosity or self indulgence. To see or to perish is the very condition laid upon everything that makes up the universe, by reason of the mysterious gift of existence. . . . I repeat that my only aim in these pages, my whole driving power, is to try to see; that is to say, to try to develop a homogeneous and coherent perspective of our general experience extended to man. A whole which unfolds. (Mooney, p. 14)

Henri de Lubac makes the important point that the person of Christ was the "dominant influence upon the elaboration of what Teilhard termed in English his 'personalistic universe.' Personalism is indeed at the heart of his system" (p. 22), leading him ultimately to conclude,

the Christ of revelation is quite simply Omega. To demonstrate this fundamental proposition, I need only refer to the long series of Johannine and especially Pauline texts where the physical supremacy of Christ over the universe is affirmed in terms which are magnificent. I cannot enumerate them here. . . . There we have the very definition of Omega. (P. 89)

They all come down to these two essential affirmations:

"He is before all things" (Col. 1:17), and "the head of every principality and power" (Col. 2:10), so that "Christ is all and in all (Col. 3:11).

Ordinarily we cannot see the air we breathe, but our life depends on it at all times. God, like the air, "encompasses us on all sides, like the world itself" (*Divine Milieu*, p. 46). The only thing that prevents us from enfolding him in your arms is your "inability to see him" (p. 46).

Reflection

By comparing the early writings of Paul to the Christian community in Rome with his later ones, it is clear that he underwent an evolution of his understanding of the mystery of Christ in relation to the created universe. The concept that the entire universe has been restored in Christ was barely hinted at in Romans 8:19–23, but a few years later, while Paul was imprisoned in Rome, it became a dominant theme in the letters to the Christian communities of Colossae and Ephesus.

✧ Take the time to review your life journey to identify those events by which Jesus has entered your life and changed its course. They are part of the unfolding of the "mystery of Christ" in your life. Jot these down in a journal so that you can come to see more clearly God's providential guidance of events in your life, even in its very details.

✧ Paul's first letter was in response to a threat to the church of Colossae, troubled by speculations on the importance of heavenly "powers" and their control of the universe and the course of events. Paul's letter to the Colossians asserts vigorously the supremacy of Christ as lord and master over the entire universe. As your own life story unfolds before you, can you identify persons and events that challenged your beliefs and practices? Did you measure up to the challenge or did you fail? If you failed did you become discouraged or did you reflect on one of Jesus' friends who also failed, perhaps many times, before coming to love Jesus who became his or her strength?

✧ Reflect that Peter, on whom Jesus ultimately founded his church, failed miserably until he came to rely not on his own powers but on the love and forgiveness of Jesus. Jesus, the patient teacher, knew that insight and strength to imple-

ment that insight are frequently a slow process, but as Morrie Schwartz, in *Tuesdays with Morrie* said, "Love always wins."

God's Word

As Jesus approached Jericho on his final trip to Jerusalem, where he would face his passion and death, a blind beggar (Luke 18:35–43), hearing the clamor of the crowd that was following Jesus as he passed by, shouted, "Jesus, Son of David, have pity on me!" Not only did he hear him, but "Jesus stopped and ordered that he be brought to him." In response to Jesus' question asking the blind man, who is called Bartimaeus in Mark's Gospel, what he wants, Bartimaeus uttered his impassioned plea, "Lord, please let me see." Twice Luke makes the point that Jesus' ministry is to bring sight to the blind. When Teilhard spoke of sight, he commonly meant insight, a usage that is similar to Luke's in which the Evangelist notes the blindness of the disciples who lacked persistence and faith compared to the blind beggar.

Saint Paul's insight into the deeper meaning of the Incarnation not only for us human beings but for all of creation has long been opaque to Christians especially in regard to the non-human created universe. In Romans 8:19–23, Saint Paul offers us an insight that clearly indicates that the whole of creation, not just humankind, has been redeemed, and that it is through human beings that redemption extends, as a result of the Incarnation, to the rest of creation.

Closing prayer: Lord Jesus, I believe what Saint Paul insisted on, that you have redeemed the whole of creation, us humans included, and that it is precisely through our bodies that redemption extends to the rest of creation. I thank you for giving to me and to all my fellow human beings a sacred "priestly" role as a missionary to the universe. Expand my vision to see that this restoration of the entire universe means that you are lord and master over the entire universe, not just over us human beings.

✧ Meditation 2 ✧

Mass on the World

Theme: The eucharistic presence of Christ was for Teilhard the symbol and concrete sign of Christ's emptying himself, so-to-speak, a "kenosis into matter" (Mooney, p. 81). Teilhard called the historical Incarnation, the sanctification of all matter in the universe and the promise of its eventual transfiguration, a Christogenesis, the universe becoming Christ!

Opening prayer: Lord Jesus, remembering that your Resurrection is the promise of my rising to eternal life, I offer up all of the events and activities of this day, my own and those of everyone around the globe. They and I share with you the humanity that you gladly came to share with us. We are your Mystical Body that we offer up with the bread of the Eucharist on your altars around the world. Take whatever achievements are ours this day as the eucharistic bread so that we may be cocreators with you in building the Earth. Take our setbacks, suffering, and diminishments of this day and pour them into the chalice of your blood that we may be coredeemers with you of the Earth and the universe.

About Teilhard

Teilhard wrote his first version of "The Mass on the World" in July 1918 in the Forest of Laigue while on leave from his duties as stretcher bearer in World War I. He had just taken his solemn vows in the Jesuit House in Lyons. His military duties often prevented him from offering Mass such as he would do under normal circumstances, so he composed a prayer that he could prayerfully recite whenever he got the opportunity.

By 1923, while on a geological expedition in the eastern Ordos Desert of China on the feast of Jesus' Transfiguration, Teilhard had developed his "Mass on the World" in its present form. Teilhard reveals how important this kind of prayer was to him during his expeditions in the field, "As I travel on mule-back for whole days on end, I repeat, as in the past—for lack of any other Mass—the 'Mass on the World'" (King, *Spirit of Fire*, pp. 102–103).

Teilhard rose from his tent in the Ordos Desert before daybreak to pray, but found that it was impossible for him to offer Mass. So he made a prayerful morning offering of the whole world, "The Mass on the World." As he looked toward the east, he saw the sun starting to rise over the mountains. He imagined the great orb of the sun as the eucharistic host, the Body of Christ, being elevated over the Earth, and thought of all the members of his Body around the world. He thought of the great mass of human beings progressively waking to the labor and achievement of the new day "who today will take up again their impassioned pursuit of the light" (*Hymn of the Universe*, p. 12). The crimson dripping sun rising over the horizon he imagined as the blood of Christ once poured out on the cross in Jerusalem, and now poured out by the members of the Mystical Body of Christ on the cross of sickness, loneliness, suffering, discrimination, and injustice wherever on the Earth the sun shines this day.

Pause: Reflect that you can offer up the "bread" of human achievement and the "wine" of human suffering as your own Mass on the world each day.

Teilhard's Words

Since once again, Lord . . . in the steppes of Asia—
I have neither bread, nor wine, nor altar, I will raise myself
beyond these symbols, up to the pure majesty of the real
itself; I, your priest, will make the whole earth my altar
and on it I will offer you all the labors and sufferings of
the world.

Over there, on the horizon, the sun has just touched
with light the outermost fringe of the eastern sky. Once
again, beneath this moving sheet of fire, the living surface
of the earth wakes and trembles, and once again begins
its fearful travail. I will place on my paten, O God, the
harvest to be won by this renewal of labor. Into my chalice I shall pour all the sap which is to be pressed out this
day from the earth's fruits.

My paten and my chalice are the depths of a soul laid
widely open to all the forces which in a moment will rise
up from every corner of the earth and converge upon the
Spirit. Grant me the remembrance and the mystic presence of all those whom the light is now awakening to the
new day. (*Hymn of the Universe*, p. 11)

Reflection

People have different ways of praying, of communing with
God. One way is by participating in the celebration of Mass.
This kind of prayer is like sharing a great book and a meal
with one you love. You can just revel in God's presence.

One of several ways of praying is by the "Morning Offering," suggested by Teilhard in the "Mass on the World." No
matter where we are each day as the sun comes over our horizon, we have a renewed opportunity to celebrate Christ's
coming to Earth to share our humanity. We have a renewed
opportunity to participate in the elevation of the Body of
Christ. We have an opportunity, like that seized by Teilhard
every morning of his life, to make our morning offering not
only of ourselves and our activities, but of the whole world.

✧ Wherever in the world you wake up in the morning, look to the east and see the rising sun, and with Teilhard's immense gratitude, love, and even heartbreak, offer your own mass on the world.

✧ Prayer can also be a communing in solidarity with those who suffer, who are ill, who experience disasters, whose lifeblood is poured out into Christ's chalice, whether they recognize it as such or not. Each of us by our heartfelt prayer can "call down the Fire" of the Holy Spirit on the world. Jesus made it clear that "whatever you do for the least of these, you do for me." Reflect on whether the love that you think you have for Jesus whom you cannot see actually enlivens you in the presence of the Christ whom you do see, the people who come within your orbit each day.

God's Word

The greatest prayer that you can offer is the eucharistic celebration in which you return in memory to the Upper Chamber in Jerusalem, the scene of Jesus' Last Supper with his friends. Hear and relish the words of Scripture and be united with and nourished by the Body and Blood, the very life of our risen Savior. Mass is meant to be a prayerful celebration, but a celebration all the same!

> The cup of blessing that we bless, is it not a participation in the blood of Christ? The bread that we break, is it not a participation in the body of Christ? Because the loaf of bread is one, we, though many, are one body, for we all partake of the one loaf. (1 Corinthians 10:16–17)

> For I received from the Lord what I also handed on to you, that the Lord Jesus, on the night he was handed over, took bread, and, after he had given thanks, broke it and said, "This is my body that is for you. Do this in remembrance of me." In the same way also the cup, after supper, saying, "This cup is the new covenant in my blood. Do this as often as you drink it, in remembrance of me." For as often as you eat this bread and drink this cup, you proclaim the death of the Lord until he comes. (1 Corinthians 11:23–27)

Closing prayer:

Receive, O Lord, this all-embracing host which your whole creation, moved by your magnetism, offers you at this dawn of a new day.

This bread, our toil, is of itself, I know, but an immense fragmentation; this wine, our pain, is no more, I know, than a draught that dissolves. . . . I will this morning climb up in spirit to the high places, bearing with me the hopes and miseries of my mother—empowered by that priesthood which you alone . . . have bestowed on me—upon all that in the world of human flesh is now about to be born or to die beneath the rising sun I will call down the Fire. (*Hymn of the Universe*, p. 13)

Cocreators of the Earth

Theme: We are called to share in building Christ's Kingdom on Earth.

Opening prayer: God, our Creator, I thank you for revealing the mystery of humanity through the Incarnation of Jesus. Teach me how to live as a cocreator with Jesus in building the Earth. Using my God-given gifts and inspirations, may I have the desire to help in building your Kingdom and the wisdom to accomplish it wisely and compassionately.

About Teilhard

Throughout World War I, Teilhard served as stretcher bearer in a mixed regiment of Moroccan light infantry and Algerian Zouaves. Although mainly at the front, he made time for prayer, reflection, and writing. In one of his letters from the front to his cousin Marguerite, Teilhard grappled with his ideas about humans cocreating with God:

> I can't believe that the world was given to man simply to *keep him busy,* as if it were a wheel to turn. There must be a precise effort to be made, a definite result to be obtained, and this must be the *axis* of human work and of human lineage, serving as the *support* or matter of our

fidelity to God, acting as the *dynamic bond* of our charity. Obviously, it's God [our Lord] who, ultimately, is all this. . . . It's evidently in the *natural perfecting* of souls, achieved by *the combined effort of all science, all aesthetic, all morality,* that we must seek a way to co-ordinate the dispersed effort of human beings. (*Making of a Mind,* pp. 181–182)

By 1918, Teilhard had sent several of his essays to his Jesuit provincial superior. The provincial and his staff were seriously troubled by the essays, especially with the two entitled "The Struggle Against the Multitude" and "Creative Union." For one thing they did not follow the theology of Saint Thomas Aquinas, at that time the only respectable guide for Catholic theology. For another they seemed to some readers to be talking about the presence of Jesus Christ in the world through love. Teilhard made clear that humans encountered Christ through science, freedom, the search, the Earth:

By helping in the spread of science and freedom, I can increase the density of the divine atmosphere, in itself as well as for me: the atmosphere in which it is always my one desire to be immersed. By laying hold of the Earth I enable myself to cling closely to you [God]. . . .

May the kingdom of matter . . . surrender to us the secrets of its texture, its movements, its history. . . .

May the race of men, grown to fuller consciousness and greater strength, become grouped into rich and happy organisms in which life shall be put to better use and bring in a hundredfold return.

May the universe offer to our gaze the symbols and forms of all harmony and all beauty.

I must *search*, and I must *find*. (*Writings in Time of War,* pp. 138–139)

Unaware that Thomas Aquinas had been accused of pantheism in his time, Teilhard's Jesuit superiors asked: Was the world then identified with Jesus Christ? Did Teilhard confuse the Creator with creatures?

This criticism marked the beginning of Teilhard's difficulties with the Vatican and led to his failure to get permission from his superiors to publish anything of a theological or spiritual nature. It also eventually led to his exile in China and in the United States, far from his beloved Paris, where he could have had a greater intellectual influence. In all this Teilhard showed obedience to his superiors and to the church. His obedience depended on his understanding of creation and divine providence. In 1924, while doing research in Mongolia, Teilhard wrote to his friend Leontine Zanta of his frustration at being suppressed and yet his determination to carry on with building the Earth. He expressed his belief that the Christian life means to communicate through fidelity with the world as consecrated by faith. He carried this conviction with him for the rest of his life. Christ is always drawing creation to himself. We cooperate by any positive action.

Teilhard's background as a geologist led him to think about the future of human evolution in terms of changes resulting from human activities, especially cerebralization or growth of consciousness. In looking at the Earth, he saw that it consists of several spheres and believed that the Earth as we know it from science may serve as a paradigm for its future evolution. The layers of the solid Earth are composed of rock. The hydrosphere, consisting of water in the ocean basins and on the surface of the Earth, supports the biosphere that is made up of a great variety of life forms. Another Earth-encircling sphere, the atmosphere, consists of air and clouds that give rise to weather and interacts with other spheres in a variety of ways. Teilhard infers that with the development of human reflection, another world-encircling sphere developed consisting of the products of mind and heart, which he called the *noosphere*, literally meaning the sphere of the mind-heart, the "thinking Earth" so to speak. Each one of us contributes to the creation of this new sphere with every exercise of our mind and heart. One of Teilhard's principal foci, where he saw exciting accumulations of the products of mind and heart, was in the pursuit of scientific research, and especially research that involved teams of researchers.

⟶   **Pause:** Ponder the fact that you are called to help build Christ's Kingdom on Earth.

Teilhard's Words

Of the two halves or components into which our lives may be divided, the most important, judging by appearances and by the price we set upon it, is the sphere of activity, endeavor and development. . . . Nothing is more certain, dogmatically, than that human action can be sanctified. "Whatever you do," says St. Paul, "do it in the name of our Lord Jesus Christ." And the dearest of Christian traditions has always been to interpret these words to mean: in intimate union with our Lord Jesus Christ. St. Paul himself, after calling upon us to "put on Christ," goes on to forge the famous series of words *collaborare, compati, commori, con-ressuscitare [to labor with, to suffer with, to die with, to rise to life with]."* . . . It is the whole of human life, down to its most 'natural' zones, which, . . . can be sanctified. (*Divine Milieu*, pp. 49–50)

Reflection

If you are to serve as one of God's worthy cocreators, you must learn first of all to face up with integrity to becoming an authentic human being. Harvey Egan (*What Are They Saying About Mysticism?*) has suggested that the basis for a future mysticism is to be found in the transcendental precepts set out by Bernard Lonergan, a significant modern Jesuit theologian. Lonergan poses the question, "Who is the authentic person?" Egan summarizes Lonergan's response, Whoever responds to the basic dynamism of the mind to be attentive, to be intelligent, to be reasonable, to be responsible, and to surrender itself in unrestricted love is an authentic person (pp. 109–110). Such responses are the answers given by the authentic person to the transcendental precepts that are given to all persons, transcending race, religion, and other personal characteristics. Lonergan and Egan agreed that before you even think about the religious dimensions of your life, you must pay attention first to what gifts you can bring to the enterprise of being an authentic human being.

✧ For you to do your part in becoming an effective instrument in God's hands, try to honestly assess what gifts have been bestowed on you by nature and by grace—these are the tools with which you will be able to work.

✧ Most of us have been given multiple gifts. However, you must look beyond what you can do and do well, to answer the question, "What is it that lights the Fire in me?" This is what Teilhard insistently spoke of—the Fire! Reflect on what energizes you and on that basis decide in what direction and to what action the Spirit is calling you.

✧ Indeed we are "God's accomplishment!" But additionally each parent, each teacher, each mentor collaborates with God, the Creator, in a real way in helping those with whom he or she comes in contact to "become God's poetry." Each one of God's collaborators makes, shapes, impresses on raw, formless, or at least not fully formed, material the stamp of one's own personality. It is true that, as Paul says in writing to the Ephesians (2:10), we are God's accomplishment, God's work of art, but it is also true that we in our time and place in the universe are collaborators with God in helping to form those who are entrusted to us by our Creator God. Reflect on the roles you have played and the people whose lives you have touched and shaped. Thank God for each of them.

✧ Years ago I became energized by the message of Saint Paul interpreted by Teilhard to mean that we can contribute to the building of that new sphere of the Earth, the noosphere. While delivering a lecture on Teilhard's spirituality, I suddenly realized that I was intensely energized by Teilhard, more so than I could have imagined. I was on Fire! I realized then the meaning of what Thomas King had said about being an "actively passive" instrument of God, a concept related to the transcendental precepts. "Teilhard believed that when Humanity spoke through him others would understand, for the same mysterious Other was also in them; by his speaking or writing the deeper identity within others would be given a voice. 'Many will understand (the mystic's) language'" (King,

Teilhard de Chardin, p. 118). Recall a time or event when you felt on fire, fully alive.

God's Word

Saint Paul describes the baptized Christians as holy, beloved and chosen by God, and says for that reason they should "clothe themselves" with a number of godlike virtues, capping them all with love that weaves them together and makes them perfect. Paul goes on to reveal that because we are members of Christ's Mystical Body, his peace must take full possession of our heart. He urges that as a result of this gift of peace, we dedicate ourselves to gratitude that will allow Christ's word, his message, his attitude, his spirit of wisdom to take life in our very being. Paul then tells us to break out in a song of gratitude in whatever way that the Holy Spirit may inspire us. And Paul commissions us to do everything in that most efficacious of all names, the Lord Jesus!

> Put on then, as God's chosen ones, holy and beloved, heartfelt compassion, kindness, humility, gentleness, and patience, bearing with one another and forgiving one another, if one has a grievance against another; as the Lord has forgiven you. . . . Over all these put on love, that is, the bond of perfection. And let the peace of Christ control your hearts. . . . And be thankful. Let the word of Christ dwell in you richly, as in all wisdom you teach and admonish one another, singing psalms, hymns, and spiritual songs with gratitude in your hearts to God. And whatever you do, in word or in deed, do everything in the name of the Lord Jesus, giving thanks to God the Father through him. (Colossians 3:12–17)

Saint Paul in writing to the Ephesians concluded the passage on the generosity of God's plan by stating, "We are God's work of art, created in Christ Jesus to lead the good life as from the beginning he meant us to live it" (Ephesians 2:10). In his autobiography, *The Letter Carrier,* William J. Leonard, commenting magnificently on the place where the liturgy and poetry meet, cites the above brief passage and comments as follows:

> Our English word "poem" is derived from [the Greek] *poiema,* and so we might understand Paul as saying, "We are God's poetry." And that reminds me of a lament of Cardinal Newman's . . . : "Alas, what are we doing all through life, both as a necessity and a duty, but unlearning the world's poetry and attaining to its prose?" "Poetry" here, I take it, meant for Newman aspiration, dreams; "prose" meant the struggle to realize and accomplish the ideal. In life we must reduce the hope and ambition to actuality; otherwise we are failures. It's a tedious process (hence "prosy"), but in the end our life again becomes poetry: every saint is a successful expression of a divine thought. To keep the metaphor, moreover, *poiein* means to make, to shape, to impress on raw, formless material one's

own personality. The image that comes to mind is that of the poet struggling to find the precise words that will express unmistakably and for the last time the concept he has in mind—crossing out, recasting, amending—the *"labor limae,"* the "drudgery of the file" that old Horace talked about. Only here it is not a human effort that is involved; Paul says that we are God's accomplishment. (P. 188)

Closing prayer: Creator God, I thank you for calling me to be an instrument of your love, a participant in bringing your Kingdom to fruition. It is you who are fashioning me by love and by fire as an instrument to help build the Earth.

✧ Meditation 4 ✧

Divinization of Our Activities

Theme: Our human actions have a value that, in part, depends on the purity of our intention. However, God has sanctified, has "divinized," all of our activities as well as all matter through the shared humanity that we hold in common with Jesus, the incarnate Word.

Opening prayer: Loving God, I am profoundly grateful for your amazing gift to me, a share in the same humanity that was assumed by your divine Son and by which all of my activities are made sacred. In union with Jesus, I am privileged to become a cocreator and coredeemer of your Kingdom in this time and place.

About Teilhard

Central to the synthesis of Teilhard's thought is Jesus' Incarnation, the insertion of the Creator of the universe into creation as a member of the human race. This unique and sacred event and its profound implications for interpreting the relationship of all other humans to Jesus, to one another, and to the entire material universe was a preoccupation of Teilhard's from at least 1916. His thought on the Incarnation and its implications was developing rapidly after his ordination to the priesthood in 1911 and during World War I. Throughout that time he served as a stretcher bearer at, and near, the battlefront, where he ministered to dying and wounded soldiers. This was a time of great growth in his thought and spirituality as evidenced by the profound ideas in his letters to his cousin Marguerite Teillard-Chambon and in some twenty essays written at the front during this time. These letters were later published in *The Making of a Mind* and the essays in *Writings in Time of War*.

By 1923 he wrote, in a somewhat lyrical fashion, a summary of the profound implications of the Incarnation for all matter in the universe:

> Once again the Fire has penetrated the earth.
>
> Not with sudden crash of thunderbolt, riving the mountain-tops: does the Master break down doors to enter his own home? Without earthquake, or thunderclap: the flame has lit up the whole world from within. All things individually and collectively are penetrated and flooded by it, from the inmost core to the tiniest atom to the mighty sweep of the most universal laws of being; so naturally has it flooded every element, every energy, every connecting link in the unity of our cosmos; that one might suppose the cosmos to have burst spontaneously into flame.
>
> In the new humanity which is begotten today the Word prolongs the unending act of his own birth; and by virtue of his immersion in the world's womb the great waters of the kingdom of matter have, without even a ripple, been endued with life. No visible tremor marks this inexpressible transformation; and yet, mysteriously and in very truth, at the touch of the supersubstantial Word the immense host which is the universe is made flesh. Through your own incarnation, my God, all matter is henceforth incarnate. (*Hymn of the Universe*, pp. 16–17)

Pause: Try to imagine the great love that God has for you that you are invited to "divinize" all the activities of your life.

Teilhard's Words

The divinisation of our endeavour by the value of the intention put into it, pours a priceless *soul* into all our actions; but *it does not confer the hope of resurrection upon their bodies.* (*Divine Milieu*, p. 55)

It is through the collaboration which he stimulates in us that Christ, starting from *all* created things, is consummated and attains his plenitude. St. Paul tells us so. We may, perhaps, imagine that the creation was finished long ago. But that would be quite wrong. It continues still more magnificently, and at the highest levels of the world. [Every created thing up to now groans and comes to birth.] And we serve to complete it, even by the humblest work of our hands. That is, ultimately, the meaning and value of our acts. Owing to the interrelation between matter, soul and Christ, we bring part of the being which he desires back to God *in whatever we do*. With each one of our *works*, we labour—in individual separation, but no less really—to build the Pleroma; that is to say, we bring to Christ a little fulfilment. (P. 62)

Reflection

Saint Paul reveals to us (Philippians 2:5–7) a great mystery, namely, that human beings are of such great dignity that Jesus chose to become one of us. Michael Himes calls Paul's statement "unquestionably the most radical statement of the dignity of the human person that has ever been made" (p. 24).

In order to experience the life-transforming effects of the Incarnation in our daily lives it is important that Jesus becomes our focal point by means of spiritual exercises. I believe that the Fire in Teilhard's thought and life was the fire of his love for the Sacred Heart of Jesus. As a Jesuit, Teilhard engaged in the spiritually aerobic exercises of Saint Ignatius that revolve around Jesus and the Holy Trinity. Teilhard was personally immersed in Jesus—he found Jesus in every activity of his life, and he brought the spirit of Christ as he had absorbed it in his prayer to every one of his activities.

The following reflection exercises can help you build an intimate relationship with Jesus. What a strong source of motivation your friendship with Jesus will bring about as you grow in intimacy with him. This incarnational perspective will divinize all of your own activities. In such meditation we assimilate the attitudes and values of Jesus, as we watch him live out the events of his life as a human being. Such prayer makes you more human and, therefore, more like God.

✧ Make your Bible a constant companion. Select a passage from the Scriptures that has special meaning for you at this time, perhaps a reading from the Mass of the day. As an example, I will use the storied account in Luke's Gospel of the Annunciation to Mary. In this passage it is clear that God intended to send his Son to become a human and that God chose Mary to be the mother who would give him birth (1:26–38).

✧ Prepare for prayer then ask for the gift that you eagerly desire from the prayer period. Reread the Scripture passage, selecting some aspect of the scene with which you resonate. You may find it helpful, for example, to reflect on Mary's being deeply troubled by the angel's greeting and see how she deals with it. You may be able to learn from Mary how you can deal with deeply troubling decisions in your own life. Mary must have foreseen complications that would quickly arise in her relationship with Joseph if she agreed to follow what the angel assured her was God's will.

✧ In this meditation, as in later formal prayer periods, begin by looking at the words, actions, and decisions of Mary and Joseph, and, once he is born, of Jesus also. Looking at implications in your own life, you will grow in your capacity for sound decision making based on your growth in thinking as Mary, as Joseph, and as Jesus did.

✧ Use the process outlined above to meditate on the varied words and actions of Jesus throughout his active life, his Passion and death, his Resurrection, and his consoling activities before ascending to heaven. I have outlined such a daily program of meditations covering twenty-four weeks on the life of Jesus (Skehan, 1991).

God's Word

Read Luke 1:26–38. Today we are at a disadvantage when we think about momentous events such as the account of God's messenger coming to Mary to ask her to become the mother of Jesus, to play a most important part in the mystery of the Incarnation. Our problem is that we know how the story turned out, and so it is easy for us to overlook the anguish and doubts that God's request caused in Mary.

She was already promised in marriage to Joseph; she was unmarried and was asked to become pregnant by the invisible most high God—how could she explain all this to Joseph? How complicated and unbelievable can a situation get? No wonder she had doubts and emotional distress! What a wonderful passage for us to meditate on as we face the day to day decisions in which we have to weigh conflicting values in our own lives as we try to make Jesus and his values and the work of his Kingdom the focal point of our lives!

Closing prayer: "Grant, Lord, that your descent into the universal Species may not be for me just something loved and cherished, like the fruit of some philosophical speculation, but may become for me truly a real Presence" that will permeate every fiber of my being and divinize the core of my every activity (*Hymn of the Universe*, p. 21).

✧ **Meditation 5** ✧

The Incarnation and the Eucharist

Theme: "We are all of us together carried in the one world-womb; yet each of us is our own little microcosm in which the incarnation is wrought independently with degrees of intensity, and shades that are incommunicable" (*Hymn of the Universe*, p. 21).

Opening prayer: Jesus, Creator and savior, how grateful I am to identify with you in your daily life as a human being in the land that we know as holy. But more than remembering you only as a historical figure, by your Incarnation, I am in intimate communion with you because you have given me the role of cocreator of the world in which I live and work.

About Teilhard

In commenting on Teilhard's first essay, "Cosmic Life," in *Writings in Time of War*, his cousin Marguerite Teillard-Chambon noted that it represented "in embryo all that was later to be developed in his thought" (p. 13). This initial period of growth in awareness took place in World War I, a time of great physical risk for Teilhard because he spent most of these years at the battlefront, ministering to wounded and dying soldiers.

The war years were for Teilhard decisive in molding his thought as to the meaning of life, both his own and that of humanity more broadly, and "the role of the Christian faith in the immense cosmic process that is the evolution of life" (King, *Spirit of Fire*, p. 53). Amazingly, almost daily he jotted down in his journal ideas that he fleshed out in essays when he had quiet time between battles.

The turmoil of war clarified his inner vision. It made him realize in a new way that matter was charged with life and with spirit. He felt so deeply, so vividly a love of matter, of life, that in later years he often used to urge his friends to trust and choose life. It was his deep-felt conviction "that *life is never mistaken*, either about its road or its destination." (P. 54)

Pause: Imagine yourself communing with God not only in meditation but through nature.

Teilhard's Words

It is first by the Incarnation and next by the Eucharist that [Christ] organizes us for himself and imposes himself upon us. . . . Although he has come above all for souls, uniquely for souls, he could not join them together and bring them life without assuming and animating along with them all the rest of the world. By his Incarnation he inserted himself not just into humanity but into the universe which supports humanity, and he did so not simply as another connected element, but with the dignity and function of a directing principle, of a Centre towards which everything converges in harmony and in love. (Mooney, pp. 70–71)

The exclusive task of the world is the physical incorporation of the faithful in the Christ, who is of God. This cardinal task is being carried out *with the rigour and harmony of a natural evolution*.

At the source of its development an operation was called for, transcendent in order, to graft the Person of a

God onto the human cosmos. . . . This was the Incarnation. . . . In virtue of the penetration of the Divine into our nature—a new life was born: grace. . . . [Grace] is the unique sap that starts from the same trunk and rises up into the branches, it is the blood that courses through the veins under the impulse of one and the same Heart, the nervous current that is transmitted through the limbs at the dictate of one and the same Head: and that radiant Head, that mighty Heart, that fruitful Stock, must inevitably be Christ. Through grace, through that single and identical life, we become much more than kinsmen, much more even than brothers: we become identified with one and the same higher Reality, which is Jesus Christ. . . .

By means of sacramental communion he consummates the union of the faithful in Himself through an individual and integral contact of soul with soul, flesh with flesh; he instills even into the matter of their being, side by side with the imperative need to adhere to the mystical Body, a seed of resurrection. . . . In the first place through the Incarnation, and then through the Eucharist, he organizes us for himself and implants himself in us. (*Writings in Time of War*, pp. 50–51)

Reflection

In his theological writings, Teilhard points out that he is simply transposing into an evolutionary framework the great cosmic affirmations of Saint Paul about the person of Christ. However, Christ for Teilhard is always the person of Jesus of Nazareth. While the Christ that Teilhard speaks of is the Christ of the Gospels, he rarely limits himself to the daily life of Christ on Earth, which he looked on as a beginning. Teilhard feels that the way to understand and grasp more fully the cosmic significance of the Incarnation is to look to its ultimate meaning. "From Christian revelation, especially . . . from the letters of St. Paul, comes belief in a cosmic function for the person of Christ by which he is Lord over all of creation" (Mooney, p. 74). "It is Jesus of Nazareth, therefore, whom Teilhard has always in mind when he identifies the Christ of revelation with the Omega of evolution" (p. 74) toward whom the universe is converging.

✧ Our faith needs to be nourished by love and especially by the consoling touch of Jesus entering our life at crucial times to enlighten us and to reveal himself to us. "When does that ever happen?" we may ask ourselves. Reflection may reveal the answer.

✧ Turn to one or other of the Gospel stories where Jesus has pity on the crowd because the people are hungry, and he and his friends feed them even though they are woefully unprepared with supplies (for example, Mark 6:30–44). Picture the people of the crowd, "like sheep without a shepherd" eager to hear the message of the weary Jesus. Using your sense of smell, imagine yourself as part of that crowd. Feel the heat made more oppressive by the dust as the crowd rushes after Jesus. As you approach the lake, imagine a refreshing breeze, hot though it is, blowing across the water and giving the crowd relief by the water's edge. Here Jesus yields to the people's eager hunger to hear his words. Listen to what Jesus is saying to you to nourish you, to strengthen you here and now as he and his friends give you nourishment for soul and body.

God's Word

One of the most heartwarming scenes in the Gospels is the appearance of the risen Jesus to his despondent friends who gave up and headed for Emmaus. Jesus, the consoler, wanted to rescue them from the despair of thinking that they had wasted time following him. Read Luke 24:13–35 in your Bible. Jesus teased the friends, instructed them, encouraged them in such a way that later they exclaimed, "Were not our hearts burning [within us] while he spoke to us on the way and opened the scriptures to us?" (verse 32). One phrase from this story is so appropriate for our own eucharistic meal: "The two recounted what had taken place on the way and how he was made known to them in the breaking of the bread" (verse 35). How important it is as you prayerfully read this and other Gospel passages to listen to Jesus, your companion for the journey, explaining his message, his values, and his desires for you. Let him nourish you with his Word, his Body and Blood, his very life, as well as with the wonderful and inspiring vision of his cosmic Body, the Earth and the universe.

Closing prayer: Lord Jesus, I thank you for implanting in the depth of my being an attraction and love that again and again surprises me, a sense of caring for all human beings and a love for the whole of the universe. I suppose it should not surprise me because I share in a bit of your infinite love poured out in a vast communion with all of the created universe. This love and yearning is a communion that nourishes my spirit at its core.

✧ **Meditation 6** ✧

Divinization of Our Passivities

Theme: We are called on to understand how God can be grasped in and through suffering, death, and setbacks.

Opening prayer: Lord Jesus, it is easy enough to understand that you can be grasped in and through every life-giving activity. But teach me how I can grasp you in diminishment, as you tried to teach your disciples on the road to Emmaus, that I, like the Messiah, must undergo all that you allow to come my way, so as to enter into your glory.

About Teilhard

Teilhard's writings about the passivities of diminishment, that is, the negative and death-dealing events that happen to us, in *The Divine Milieu* are eloquent and contain powerful reasons for accepting these things. Throughout his personal and professional life, Teilhard experienced more than the normal number and kinds of setbacks, disappointments, and sorrows. Seven of his eleven siblings died before him, including his brothers Oliver and Gonzague, who died in the war; his sister Françoise, who died in Shanghai in 1911 as superior of the Little Sisters of the Poor; and his invalid sister Marie, with whom he had a special bond. Upon her death in 1936 he wrote, "Her loss has created a sort of universal solitude around me, that affects all the aspects of an interior world of which I had gradually made her a part" (De Lubac, p. 5).

In his work, directives that came indirectly from the Vatican through his superiors blocked him from publishing his essays on religion and spirituality. The suppression of his work was not merely annoying but cut to the heart of what he considered was the mission for which he was uniquely well prepared. Since that time his writings, published after his death in 1955, have received wide and enthusiastic acceptance, including words of praise from Cardinal Agostino Casaroli in 1981 who wrote in the name of our Holy Father, Pope John Paul II (*Origins*, 16 July, 1981).

Teilhard lived in repressive and turbulent times. As a Jesuit scholastic, he and his fellow seminarians lived and studied on the Isle of Jersey because they were exiles from France during a repressive government regime that drove out many religious men and women. From the turn of the twentieth century to the 1940s, authorities in the Catholic church, in their concern for doctrinal rigor, had such strict norms for publication that Teilhard's writings failed to pass muster. This was the case until after his death, when the windows of the church were opened by the Holy Spirit and Pope John XXIII convened the Second Vatican Council.

It is a testament to Teilhard's faith and fidelity to his perceived mission that he continued to write his essays and books for some forty years, with limited opportunity for publication in French and essentially no possibility of publication in English. Some of his more influential peers, distressed by the suppression of his manuscripts, urged him to leave the Jesuit order and the church. He would then be free to publish his many and exciting Scripture-based essays that shed new light on Christ's Incarnation and on human participation in the work of the Kingdom. Trusting in the guidance of the Holy Spirit and maintaining his fidelity to the Jesuit and Catholic way of life to which he had committed himself, Teilhard practiced what he preached in terms of "divinization of his passivities." Although Teilhard was thinking of death in the following passage, what he says is equally applicable to dashed hopes and impending death of his brain children: "We must overcome death by finding God in it. And by the same token, we shall find the divine established in our innermost hearts, in the last stronghold which might have seemed able to escape his reach" (*Divine Milieu,* p. 82).

Pause: In reflecting on Teilhard's many setbacks and sufferings, imagine how you may react to events that afflict you, especially the untimely death of loved ones or of your brain children.

Teilhard's Words

When the signs of age begin to mark my body (and still more when they touch my mind); when the ill that is to diminish me or carry me off strikes from without or is born within me; when the painful moment comes in which I suddenly awaken to the fact that I am ill or growing old; and above all at that last moment when I feel I am losing hold of myself and am absolutely passive within the hands of the great unknown forces that have formed me; in all those dark moments, O God, grant that I may understand that it is you (provided only my faith is strong enough) who are painfully parting the fibres of my being in order to penetrate to the very marrow of my substance and bear me away within yourself. (*Divine Milieu,* pp. 89–90)

Reflection

The only way to make sense of your human sufferings, setbacks, death, and burial is in sharing them in solidarity with Jesus. Because you share the same humanity as Jesus, you also share today as coredeemer in Jesus' role as redeemer. The passion and death of Jesus make sense in terms of his Resurrection from the dead to eternal life. His Resurrection is also the promise of your resurrection. While you are called to live in the modern culture and to share your learning and your life with other human beings, you are at the same time called by Jesus to live that life by Christ's standards and values. In certain situations in your everyday life, you may discover that Jesus' values are countercultural and, therefore, if you are to be an authentic Christian, an authentic human being, you will be called upon to follow Christ's values—to be a Christian.

✧ You can learn how to more securely make Christ's values your own, especially when diminishments come to you unsought and undesired, by following a method that Teilhard used throughout his life. He regularly meditated on the life, passion, death, and Resurrection of Jesus and so assimilated Christ's values into his everyday life, especially when he experienced setbacks and disappointments, which were numerous and followed him throughout his otherwise exciting life. He followed the spiritual exercises of Ignatius of Loyola, founder of the Jesuit order of which Teilhard was a loyal and distinguished member.

✧ Like Teilhard, we can seek a new level of intimacy with Jesus in our prayer periods by meditating on the Gospel accounts of Jesus' passion. The Gospel narratives of the Last Supper, John 13:1–30, Matthew 26:20–30, and Mark 14:10–26, are a good starting point. Approach each period by properly preparing and seeking the grace or gift that you want, as well as the colloquy or intimate conversation or communion flowing out of the prayer. Include the following three practices in each meditation:

✦ See the persons in the Gospel passage as vividly as possible in the scene described.
✦ Hear what they are saying, not just the words, but the attitude and emotion implicit in what they say.
✦ Observe what they are doing.

In addition, let your heart and imagination suggest additional details that may be consistent with, and help to make more vivid, the entire scene.

Three additional guidelines will help you to energize your prayer concerned with Jesus' diminishment:

✦ Make an even greater effort to labor with Christ in his anguish, his struggle, his suffering, or what he desires to suffer.

✦ When praying the passion passages, pay special attention to how the divinity hides itself so that Jesus seems utterly human and helpless.

✦ In realizing that Christ loves you so much that he willingly suffers everything for your rejections and sins, ask yourself, "What can I, in response, do for him?"

It is of utmost importance that in prayer you direct your involvement away from yourself in order to focus on compassionate communion with Jesus' suffering before your very eyes. The tendency will be to recoil from true compassion knowing that your sinfulness is intimately bound up with Jesus' suffering. Compassionate union with Jesus will soften and break whatever in your heart needs healing and strengthening.

God's Word

As Jesus was starting to impress upon his followers the price he had to pay for speaking out clearly the messianic message that he had been sent on Earth to proclaim, Peter, in his love for his leader, would have none of it. After all this time together, Peter still did not understand that suffering, setbacks, and even death would be that price. Jesus knew that he had to go to Jerusalem and so spoke strongly, if not in anger, because Peter still had not gotten his core message. Long after Jesus' suffering, death, and Resurrection, Peter did come to realize that he too must finally embrace the cross:

> Then he strictly ordered his disciples to tell no one that he was the Messiah.
>
> From that time on, Jesus [the Messiah] began to show his disciples that he must go to Jerusalem and suffer greatly from the elders, the chief priests, and the scribes, and be killed and on the third day be raised. Then Peter took him aside and began to rebuke him, "God forbid, Lord! No such thing shall ever happen to you." He turned and said to Peter, "Get behind me, Satan! You are an obstacle to me. You are thinking not as God does, but as human beings do." (Matthew 16:20–23)

Closing prayer: Lord God, "after having perceived you as he who is 'a greater myself,' grant, *when my hour comes,* that I may recognise you under the species of each alien or hostile force that seems bent on destroying or uprooting me" (*Divine Milieu,* p. 89).

✧ Meditation 7 ✧

Finding God in All Things

Theme: Because of Jesus' Incarnation, all matter in the universe has become sacred, and all of our activities partake of the sacred. As a result the distinction between the sacred and the profane fades away. Cultivating a spirit of reverence will allow us to strive for Ignatius's goal to "seek and find God in all things."

Opening prayer: Lord Jesus, throughout your life on Earth, and still today through the quiet activity of the Holy Spirit, you went about curing the blind. And in your teaching, you have helped us to see, to be able to find God in every facet of our lives, and in all the created universe.

About Teilhard

Teilhard wrestled from childhood with a problem that is at least as old as human existence: how to reconcile "the discontinuity that he experienced between the love of God and love of the world, between human achievement and the kingdom of Christ, between Christian detachment and personal self-development, between the data of revelation and scientific research" (Mooney, p. 13). Teilhard's lifelong preoccupation was a search for unity between his two loves, God and the world. The fire of his love for God led him to embrace a call to religious life, to the study of philosophy and theology that, in time, brought him to priesthood in the Jesuit order. His love of the world led him first to revel in exploring nature as an enthusiastic naturalist and amateur geologist. Later, as a professional paleontologist, he explored the parade of life recorded by fossils in the rock formations of various ages. His geological excursions took him over large parts of the world, from western Europe to Tibet and China, from Java to South Africa and North America, where he explored the broader aspects of Earth's evolution with special discoveries of the early history of the human family.

Teilhard's essay "My Universe" provides us with some idea of his fundamental tendency, or innate disposition, his cast of mind that ultimately led him into a particular way of seeing everything, whether earthly or divine.

> However far back I go into my memories . . . I can distinguish in myself the presence of a strictly dominating passion: the passion for the Absolute. . . .
>
> Ever since my childhood, the need to lay hold of 'some Absolute' in everything was the axis of my inner life. I can remember very vividly that, for all my youthful pleasures, I was happy only *in terms of* a fundamental delight; and that consisted generally in the possession, or the thought of, some more precious, rarer, more consistent, more immutable object. At one time it would be a piece of metal; at another, I would take a leap to the other extreme and find satisfaction in the thought of God-the-Spirit. . . .
>
> This may well seem an odd preoccupation. I can only repeat that it was a fact, and a *permanent* fact. I was never to be free from the irresistible (and at the same time vitalizing and soothing) need to find *unending* rest in Some Thing that was tangible and *definitive*; and I sought everywhere for this blissful object.
>
> The story of my inner life is the story of this search, directed upon continually more universal and more perfect realities. . . .
>
> Since my childhood, and in later days ever more fully and with a greater sense of conviction, I have always

loved and sought to read the face of Nature; . . . It seems to me that every effort I have made, even when directed to a purely natural object, has always been a religious effort: substantially, it has been one single effort. At all times, and in all I have done, I am conscious that my aim has been to attain the Absolute. I would never, I believe, have had the courage to busy myself for the sake of any other end.

Science (which means all forms of human activity) and Religion have always been for me one and the same thing: both have been, so far as I have been concerned, the pursuit of one and the same Object. (*Heart of Matter*, pp. 197–198)

It seems clear that Teilhard's lifelong search for "the Absolute" was his path to finding God in all things as Saint Ignatius urged those who engaged in his exercises to do. Teilhard grappled, and I think successfully, with a fundamental dichotomy of human existence: it is natural enough for us to accept and understand how good things happen to us humans; how can we understand and accept "bad things" that happen to us, especially those that are not of our causing? A principal focal point of *The Divine Milieu* deals with finding God in all of the events of one's life, whether experiencing the divinization of activities of accomplishment or the divinization of passivities of diminishment. Teilhard wrote this classic little volume, devoted to living in "God's environment" or in "the divine milieu," during a period of great personal heartbreak from 1926 to 1927 when he was banished from France to China.

⟶ **Pause:** Are you energized by the thought that your activity is bringing "to Christ a little fulfilment"?

Teilhard's Words

How can the man who believes in heaven and the Cross continue to believe seriously in the value of worldly occupations? How can the believer, in the name of everything that is most Christian in him, carry out his duty as a man to the fullest extent and as whole-heartedly and freely as if he were on the direct road to God? (*Divine Milieu*, p. 51)

[E]very man, in the course of his life must not only show himself docile and obedient. By his fidelity, he must *build*—starting with the most natural territory of his own self—a work, an *opus*, into which something enters from all the elements of the earth. He *makes his own soul throughout all his earthly days*, and at the same time he collaborates in another work, in another *opus*, which infinitely transcends, while at the same time it narrowly determines, the perspectives of his individual achievement: the completing of the world. (Pp. 60–61)

Reflection

The author of the phrase, Finding God in all things, was Fr. Jeronimo Nadal, companion and biographer of Saint Ignatius. Nadal was impressed with the ease with which Ignatius found God in all things. What he meant is that:

"He found God not only in quiet prayer, but also in the confused messiness of his daily work, with all its problems and concerns, as well as in his ordinary conversations with others. So it happens that the ideal and final objective Ignatius proposed to his followers, "finding God in all things," constituted his own inner attitude. Referring to this inner attitude, Nadal got to the essential idea when he summed it up this way: . . . "He followed the Spirit who led him, he did not go before it." (Buckley, p. 584)

Thomas King, in the preface to his book *Teilhard's Mysticism of Knowing*, points out that Teilhard was familiar with a form of the mysticism of "unknowing" but "questioned the experience until it 'reversed' and he began to develop a mysticism of knowing—particularly as knowing relates to scientific discovery"(p. vii). King makes this significant statement:

I now believe the real significance of Teilhard is not that he might have reconciled truths of modern science with the truths of Christian faith, nor that he was a Christian mystic with a considerable scientific achievement (several hundred published articles); rather, it is in Teilhard's exuberant claim that in the very act of scientifically achieving, he knew God. Teilhard began writing a theology of process and many of his readers came to see as he had seen; for when human knowledge is in process, God is found in the act of knowing." (P. vii)

✦ Reflect on your frame of mind as you go about your work. In order for you to discover whether you are finding God in what you are doing, ask yourself: "Am I being energized by it or getting satisfaction from the activity as it is in process?" What you are doing may be difficult or distasteful, but if you recognize that it is something that you ought to do for the sake of love, you are probably finding God in it.

✦ You may at times be anxious if you cannot come to a firm decision quickly about what is next in your life. To use Saint Thomas's metaphor, recall that in God's providential care, you are an arrow in flight. You may not know where you are headed, but the divine Archer knows and has launched you on a course where you can be most effective, whether you know it or not.

God's Word

Job, a devout, rich chieftain of great integrity, suddenly suffers incredible losses including a devastating disease that afflicts his body, and he becomes depressed. But he does not complain against God, although when friends come to console him, he protests that he is innocent of wrongdoing and does not understand why he is so afflicted.

Job curses the day of his birth and hopes that death will bring his sufferings to an end, and he asks for a response from God. In the end Job pleads that he be allowed to see and hear from God the cause of his suffering. God answers him, not by justifying God's actions before Job's friends but by referring to God's own omniscience and almighty power. Job is satisfied by God's response and recovers his attitude of humility and trust in God, which has been intensified and strengthened by his struggle with suffering.

Although the author of the Book of Job is unknown, it appears that it was composed about twenty-five hundred years ago. "Job lives within a *tribal* culture. He is patriarch of the tribe. . . . Family ties are close. . . . Tribal culture is an *oral* one. . . . Predominantly a *shame* culture. . . . Honor and shame are pivotal values" (Bergant and Karris, p. 676). When Job's friends attributed his losses and sufferings to his wrongdoing, it was unjust and an almost unbearable loss of honor, an almost insuperable test of his fidelity. Nevertheless he was faithful to the end. The lesson of this literary and spirituality masterpiece is that even the just may suffer and that their sufferings are a test of their faithfulness.

After a long series of trials, discussions, and speeches by Job and his friends, Job speaks of wisdom in comparison to riches from the Earth:

> There is indeed a mine for silver,
>> and a place for gold which men refine.
> Iron is taken from the earth,
>> and copper is melted out of stone.
>
> . . . .
>
> But whence can wisdom be obtained,
>> and where is the place of understanding?
> Man knows nothing to equal it,
>> nor is it to be had in the land of the living.
> Solid gold cannot purchase it,
>> nor can its price be paid with silver.
>
> . . . .
>
> God knows the way to it,
>
> . . . .
>
> And to man he said:
>> Behold the fear of the LORD is wisdom;
>>> and avoiding evil is understanding."
>
> (Job 28:1–28)

Job's friends, by many arguments, finally conclude that his misfortunes resulted from wrongdoing; Job protests his innocence and God's all-knowing goodness. At length as his sufferings come to an end, Job's fidelity is vindicated. (See Job 42:1–8.)

Closing prayer: Lord God, grant that I may leave my mark on your world as cocreator and coredeemer with you by offering to you, and so divinizing, my activities as well as those things that happen to me over which I have no control. Instill in me more fully each day a spirit of reverence by which I may more successfully strive to achieve Ignatius's goal of "seeking and finding God in all things."

✧ **Meditation 8** ✧

Discovering Your Divine Milieu

Theme: "'Omnipresence' is indeed the central theme of the whole work" [*The Divine Milieu*], and the title itself is a synonym for the presence of Christ, who "'through his humanity' is the active Centre radiating all those energies which lead the universe back to God" (Mooney, p. 80).

Opening prayer: God, our Creator, you are present everywhere at all times. Give me the eyes to perceive your divine omnipresence even as I recognize your handiwork in the universe so that I may thereby come to know you more intimately, love you more ardently, and so respond generously to your invitation to join you in the great adventure of working energetically for the coming of your Kingdom.

About Teilhard

In 1924 Teilhard was reproached by the Holy Office of the Vatican through the Jesuit authorities in Rome for his far-reaching speculations in a draft of a paper on original sin. In this manuscript, which he prepared reluctantly at the request of one of his colleagues, Teilhard made note of difficulties with the traditional doctrine of original sin and suggested other possible ways of understanding original sin. As a result in 1925 Teilhard was ordered into exile, banished from his native France, to return to Tientsin, China, in disgrace. After arriving in China at Easter 1926, he set out for three months of fieldwork near the China-Tibet border after which he began writing his most famous book on Christian spirituality, *The Divine Milieu*.

The period from November 1926 to December 1927 was a time of intense reflective activity that served as both a *center* and an *environment* of transfiguration, a *milieu*. This concept of a milieu held a lifelong fascination for Teilhard. "For Teilhard the idea of the 'divine milieu' was particularly important in capturing the universal influence of Christ through God's incarnation in the world, in its matter, life, and energy—an extended, cosmic understanding of the incarnation that far transcended the historical limitations of time and place associated with the person of Jesus" (King, *Spirit of Fire*, p. 110). He finished writing the *The Divine Milieu* in 1927. The orthodoxy of the text was acknowledged, but its publication was forbidden and delayed until 1957. For those thirty years between writing and publication, manuscript copies were circulated privately and widely.

Pause: Try to imagine your own reaction to authority in the face of severe criticism or even exile from your native land.

Teilhard's Words

As Teilhard was composing "his little book," he wrote, "I want to write it slowly, quietly—living it and meditating on it like a prayer" (*Letters from a Traveller*, pp. 133–134).

Additionally, Ursula King notes that "like so many of Teilhard's writings, *The Divine Milieu* is born out of a practical, pastoral concern. He poses the problem of how Christians can best sanctify action and what value all human endeavor has in relation to God" (*Spirit of Fire*, p. 113). Teilhard's twofold answer, "'the divinization of activities' and 'the divinization of passivities' represent a continuous process of transformation whereby we can find communion with God in the world"

(p. 113). She notes that it contains "some wonderful passages that speak of our passivities of growth as well as those of diminishment, about attachment and detachment, the transfiguration of our failures, the meaning of the cross, and the spiritual power of matter" (p. 113).

As Teilhard explores the nature of the divine milieu, the universal Christ, and the Great Communion, he breaks out in a long colloquy that focuses on his need (and ours) not only to love but to adore:

> Sometimes people think that they can increase your attraction in my eyes by stressing almost exclusively the charm and goodness of your human life in the past. But truly, O Lord, if I wanted to cherish only a man, then I would surely turn to those whom you have given me in the allurement of their present flowering. Are there not, with our mothers, brothers, friends and sisters, enough irresistibly lovable people around us? Why should we turn to Judaea two thousand years ago? No, what I cry out for, like every being, with my whole life and all my earthly passion, is something very different from an equal to cherish: it is a God to adore.
>
> To adore . . . that means to lose oneself in the unfathomable, to plunge into the inexhaustible, to find peace in the incorruptible, to be absorbed in defined immensity, to offer oneself to the fire . . . and to give of one's deepest to that whose depth has no end. Whom, then, can we adore?
>
> The more man becomes man, the more will he become prey to a need, a need that is always more explicit, more subtle and more magnificent, the need to adore. (*Divine Milieu*, pp. 127–128)

Teilhard points out that in our divine milieu

> we recognise an omnipresence which acts on us by assimilating us [in the unity of the Body of Christ]. As a consequence of the Incarnation, the divine immensity has transformed itself for us into *the omnipresence of christification*. All the good that I can do . . . is physically gathered in, by something of itself, into the reality of the consum-

mated Christ. Everything I endure, with faith and love, by way of diminishment or death, makes me a little more closely an integral part of his mystical body. (P. 123)

Reflection

God's presence, God's omnipresence assimilates me in the unity of God's body, a unity by which I am 'Christified.' Grant that I may have a share in making more visible the presence of Christ that has silently been growing in things (Mooney, p. 80).

✦ Recall a time when you had to make a choice about leaving or staying. What guided you? What was the result?

✦ When have you felt constrained by a web of difficulties and disappointments? How did God transform you through that experience?

God's Word

Read Luke 7:18–23. Isn't it consoling for us whose ability to recognize the "real" Jesus may be limited, to know from Luke's Gospel that John the Baptist, who had the advantage of knowing Jesus face to face and had heard that he worked miracles, still wasn't sure whether Jesus was "he who is to come"—meaning the Messiah! John had been confined to prison (Luke 3:20), but his followers kept him informed about Jesus' ministry. Now he sends them to ask Jesus point blank, "Are you 'He who is to come' or do we look for someone else?" a consecrated phrase meaning the Messiah (Malachi 3:1), or a Moses-like figure (Deuteronomy 18:15) with whom both Jesus and John were linked in the popular mind.

Why did John doubt that Jesus was the one? John, having heard stories of Jesus' compassion, love, and forgiveness, apparently did not recognize in him an end time kind of leader, someone he envisioned as severely judgmental and described as "one mightier than I" (Luke 3:16). John's followers arrived in time to observe Jesus' healing ministry. When questioned, Jesus responded to John's question by telling them, "Go and tell John what you have seen and heard: The blind regain their sight, the lame walk, lepers are cleansed, the deaf hear, the dead are raised, the poor have the good news proclaimed to them. And blessed is the one who takes no offense at me" (Luke 7:22–23). This is not only an obvious reference to Israel's deliverance (Isaiah 29:18–19; 35:4–6, "Here is your God") but a warning that even John may find in Jesus a stumbling block and that he could block God's plan if he is not ready to accept what is for him a surprise.

Closing prayer: Jesus, I have come to realize through Teilhard's insights that when you come to me sacramentally in the Eucharist, it is not only to hold conversation with me but to join me more and more to yourself physically because your Incarnation is realized in me through the Eucharist. I am privileged to see that you are the center of my universe as well as the environment—the milieu in which "I have been taken possession of by Christ" (Philippians 3:12). You are not only my personal center, but a transcendent center that activates the love energy of the world (Mooney, p. 74).

Communion
Through Action

Theme: We share in a communion with Jesus through our action as cocreators and coredeemers in our time and place.

Opening prayer:

> Grant, O God, that when I draw near to the altar to communicate, I may henceforth discern the infinite perspectives hidden beneath the smallness and nearness of the Host in which you are concealed. I have already accustomed myself to seeing, beneath the stillness of that piece of bread, a devouring power which, in the words of the greatest doctors of the Church, far from being consumed by me, consumes me. . . .
>
> . . . I shall . . . *react* to the eucharistic contact with the *entire effort of my life*. (*Divine Milieu*, p. 126)

About Teilhard

To appreciate the wellspring that was the source of *The Divine Milieu*, we need to empathize with Teilhard during his woundedness and his healing while he was writing it. It is a rare person who has never experienced setbacks and disappointments, to a greater or lesser disgrace, real or imagined. Teilhard discovered the passivities of diminishment in his dedicated efforts to assist others to know, love, and serve Christ through his insightful writings. Imagine his distress and his feelings of betrayal by those who, one would have thought, should be most supportive of new ways of knowing and relishing God's activity in the hearts of Christians that Teilhard was unveiling. In the end Teilhard obeyed his superiors and went into exile in Tientsin, China, but only after he had been tempted, and vigorously encouraged by some of his colleagues, to leave the Society of Jesus. He came to recognize in his own heart "that it was only through the Church and his order that he could live and grow in that particular spiritual life that he had chosen as his special vocation," his own divine milieu (King, *Spirit of Fire*, p. 108).

Teilhard's exile to China allowed him to carry out a fruitful career of scientific discovery beyond his wildest dreams by means of his geological studies, but his faith was severely tested as obstacles to his work there sprang up over the decades. Teilhard's friend and defender, Henri de Lubac, SJ, later Cardinal de Lubac, observed that Teilhard's life "was dogged by external difficulties and disappointments which formed an almost endless web around him" (King, *Spirit of Fire*, pp. 108–109). He was personally strengthened by his advice given to others, "We must 'cherish, along with fulfillments of our life, everything that diminishes us, that is to say, all the passive purifications which Christ has planned for us in order to transform into himself those elements of our personality which we seek to develop for him'" (Mooney, p. 116).

Pause: Your path to Jesus may be different from that of others, but it must be by communion or love of him. Is yours a path of active service or a communion of passivities or suffering?

Teilhard's Words

In speaking about communion through action, Teilhard says:

> Each one of our works, by its more or less remote or direct effect upon the spiritual world, helps to make perfect Christ in his mystical totality. That is the fullest possible answer to the question: How can we, following the call of St. Paul, see God in all the active half of our lives? In fact, through the unceasing operation of the Incarnation, the divine so thoroughly permeates all our creaturely energies that, in order to meet it and lay hold on it, we could not find a more fitting setting than that of our action.
>
> To begin with, in action I adhere to the creative power of God; I coincide with it; I become not only its instrument but its living extension. And as there is nothing more personal in a being than his will, I merge myself, in a sense, through my heart, with the very heart of God. . . .
>
> The soul does not pause to relish this communion; . . . for it is wedded to a *creative* effort. The will to succeed, a certain passionate delight in the work to be done, form an integral part of our creaturely fidelity. . . .
>
> . . . Any increase that I can bring upon myself or upon things is translated into some increase in my power to love and some progress in Christ's blessed hold upon the universe. Our work appears to us, in the main, as a way of earning our daily bread. But its essential virtue is on a higher level: through it we complete in ourselves the subject of the divine union; and through it again we somehow make to grow in stature the divine term of the one with whom we are united, our Lord Jesus Christ. Hence whatever our role . . . may be, whether we are artists, working-men or scholars, we can, if we are Christians, speed toward the object of our work as though towards an opening on to the supreme fulfillment of our beings. (*Divine Milieu*, pp. 62–63)

Reflection

Teilhard's reflections are commonly cosmic in their scope, but he often applies the cosmic to his own life, as he seems to have done here in the discussion of communion through action. In the following closing prayer, Teilhard speaks cryptically of his "life which seemed, a few minutes ago, like a baptism with you in the waters of the world." Here he appears to refer to his having been banished in disgrace to China by his Jesuit superiors at the behest of the Vatican because of his written views on original sin. Christian Baptism has traditionally carried with it the symbolism of burial in baptismal waters with Christ who was buried in the tomb. Teilhard's Baptism with Jesus in the waters of the world conveys something of the death that he died in being banished from France, but his resurrection seems to have been complete: "It was a joy to me, O God, in the midst of the struggle, to feel that in developing myself I was increasing the hold that you have upon me" (*Divine Milieu*, p. 89).

The late William J. Leonard, SJ, professor of liturgy at Boston College, who was much involved in liturgical renewal before and after Vatican Council II, comments on God's action in our lives: God is in communion with us and we with God in our liturgical worship in the sacraments. This two-way communion extends to all of the "sacraments," whether part of the created world or products of the creative energy of members of the Mystical Body of Christ. In a way analogous to the sacraments, the universe is filled with those people and objects in nature that point to the Creator of them all, so that we can be inspired to praise God's glory, a most exalted kind of action as well as communion.

✧ Reflect on your understanding of the church's liturgy and your experience of it. It has been said, "God's shaping hands are the fashioning liturgy of the Church, by which, to be sure, we worship him, but by which, also he molds us to the likeness of his Son" (Leonard, p. 189).

✧ What has the sacrament of Baptism meant in your daily personal life? When you are at Mass or at other times during the day, do you reflect on what it means that you are said to have received the Holy Spirit or that you share in some way in the priesthood of Christ?

God's Word

Saint Paul's letter to the Ephesians (1:3–23) expresses gratitude to God for revealing the cosmic importance of Christ's Incarnation and his role as head of all creation to each person. Paul prays that they be given the spirit of wisdom and revelation.

> Blessed be the God and Father of our Lord Jesus Christ, who has blessed us in Christ with every spiritual blessing in the heavens, as [God] chose us . . . before the foundation of the world, to be holy and without blemish. . . . In love [God] destined for adoption . . . Jesus Christ, in accord with the favor of [God's] grace . . . granted us in the beloved. (Ephesians 1:3–6)

Paul goes on to express the centrality of the Incarnation and Christ's role as head or center of *all* creation (vv. 7–10). It seems clear that Paul is praising the Ephesians for their part in building up Christ's Mystical Body, and praying for them to persevere in adversity.

Closing prayer: Grant that my life may

> become, as a result of the sacrament, an unlimited and endless contact with you—that life which seemed, a few moments ago, like a baptism with you in the waters of the world, now reveals itself to me as communion with you through the world. It is the sacrament of life. *The sacrament of my life*—of my life received, of my life lived, of my life surrendered. (*Divine Milieu*, pp. 126–127)

The Face of Love

Theme: "The world's energies and substances . . . produced the glittering gem of matter, the Pearl of the Cosmos, and the link with the incarnate personal Absolute—the Blessed Virgin Mary, Queen and Mother of all things" (*Writings in Time of War*, p. 59).

Opening prayer: Mary, my mother, may we, all generations of the human race, grow in wisdom and love of you.

About Teilhard

As Teilhard set about developing a coherent and comprehensive synthesis of his thoughts on the "Eternal Feminine," it was inevitable that he would focus on love, as did the Evangelist John. He dedicated his essay on the Eternal Feminine to Beatrix, an obvious allusion to Dante's name for the girl who was the love of his life. In this essay Teilhard developed his concept of the role of love in the universe as the force that unifies and spiritualizes beings.

Teilhard came out of service at the end of World War I not only unscathed, without wounds or disability, but also greatly matured and with much to be thankful for, especially a life of adventure and freedom from care. His correspondence from 1914 through 1918 was preserved by Marguerite Teilhard-

Chambon in *Letters from a Traveller* and edited under her pen
name Claude Aragonnes. Many of Teilhard's emerging ideas
on spirituality, and especially those on one of his favorite topics, the Eternal Feminine, were recorded there and in his book
written during these years, *Writings in Time of War*.

Pause: Remember that Mary was a Jewish village woman
of faith, and gain courage in your efforts to bring God to birth
in your own world.

Teilhard's Words

For me the Immaculate Conception is the feast of "passive
action," the action that functions simply by the transmis-
sion through us of divine energy. . . . In our Lord, all
modes of lower, restless, activity disappear within this
single, luminous function of drawing God to oneself. . . .
To be active in such a way and such a degree, Our Lady
must have been brought into existence in the very heart
of grace. . . . May our Lord give you and me too, a little
of her translucence, which is so favourable to God's action." (*Making of a Mind*, p. 149)

8th December 1918 [Feast of the Immaculate Conception]
You know what . . . is my dearest wish: that God,
through our Lady, may grant us so to share in her purity . . . that we may really be able to serve, in our own
small way, to regenerate the world. (P. 262)

God created the Virgin Mary, that is to say he called forth
on earth a purity so great that, within this transparency,
he would concentrate himself to the point of appearing as
a child. There, expressed in its strength and reality, is the
power of purity to bring the divine to birth among us.
    And yet the Church, addressing the Virgin Mother,
adds: [Blessed are you who have believed]. For it is in
faith that purity finds the fulfilment of its fertility. (*Divine
Milieu*, p. 134)

Reflection

Dante is one of the greatest authors of our Christian classics because like Teilhard de Chardin, he gets to the heart of the matter of what the Christian life is all about. The leitmotif of Dante's *The New Life* and *The Divine Comedy* portrays our lives as a vision, a journey, a healing, a transformation through the gift of divine love, and finally a home. This may become a fearful and unexpected journey as we become pilgrim exiles traveling to Paradise, our true homeland.

✧ Reflect on the suggestion that a way to envision Mary is as "friend of God and prophet within the communion of saints" (Johnson, p. 8). This way of thinking places Marian teaching squarely within the Second Vatican Council's and subsequent teaching on the church, and means that Mary, as a poor Jewish village woman of faith, is "a partner in hope in the company of all graced women and men who have gone before us" (p. 13).

✧ Because Mary was a person of faith, she found herself in a partnership role with God to bring to fulfillment the birth of the messianic king. If you are nourished by a strong faith, you too can help bring Christ to birth in the hearts and minds of your companions on the journey.

God's Word

The theme of the first part of Teilhard's essay "The Eternal Feminine," is taken from Proverbs 8:22–31. Here Wisdom is personified as the first born of the Lord's new creation. Just as the church has selected the Proverbs passage for a reading in the Mass for a feast of Mary, Teilhard applies it to the Eternal Feminine, the Essential Feminine. In extending the thought in the Proverbs passage to the Eternal Feminine and to Wisdom personified, Teilhard writes, "He who takes me, gives himself to me, and is himself taken by the universe" (*Writings in Time of War*, p. 195). His footnote explains his meaning, namely, that "there is more in human love than two beings seeking to be made one. It entails, for them, contact with the whole of the universe and participation in the work of creation" (p. 195).

Closing prayer: "Praised be the God, . . . who has bestowed on us in Christ every spiritual blessing in the heavens! God chose us in him before the world began, to be holy and blameless in his sight, to be full of love; likewise he predestined us through Christ Jesus to be his adopted sons and daughters" (Ephesians 1:3–6; second reading, Mass of the Immaculate Conception).

The Sacred Heart of Jesus on Fire

Theme: Jesus' universal presence spfings forth from his Sacred Heart in a blaze that is at once diaphany and fire (*Heart of Matter*, p. 58).

Opening prayer: "Heart of Jesus, give me a heart that is filled with ardor and generosity, that thrills with joy when sacrifices have to be made; a heart whose zeal knows neither fatigue nor obstacles; a heart whose only love is your heart, and whose only knowledge is your name" (prayer of Françoise Teilhard de Chardin, in King, *Spirit of Fire*, p. 33).

About Teilhard

Teilhard's spirituality and his orientation toward science have their roots in his family. Teilhard's mother, Berthe-Adèle had an ardent devotion to the Sacred Heart of Jesus that was nourished daily by meditation. On more than one occasion, Teilhard payed her a heartfelt tribute suggesting that he owed to her the best of his thought. Teilhard was especially devoted to his sisters, Marguerite-Marie, an invalid for many years, and Françoise.

Henri de Lubac understood Teilhard's desire not only to harmonize his Christian faith and science but also to integrate his work and prayer so as to achieve a coherence. De Lubac wrote explanations of Teilhard's theological and philosophical writings that paved the way for their widespread acceptance within the Catholic church. He helped to clarify that Teilhard's Christology was not only traditional but that his perspective on "the cosmic Christ" and the "ever greater Christ" and similar ways of perceiving Christ were based in many cases on new orthodox insights into the writings of Saint Paul and Saint John the Evangelist.

> This "ever-greater Christ" was, again, the Sacred Heart, devotion to whom he had learnt from his mother, and to whom he sometimes used to address the prayer of an old sixteenth-century Jesuit: ["I beg you, Lord, to place me in the innermost recesses of your Heart!"] In the Sacred Heart he found "above all the Master of the spiritual life," and of the Sacred Heart he wrote to his cousin in 1917: "Our Lord's heart is indeed ineffably beautiful and satisfying: it exhausts all reality and answers all the soul's needs. The very thought of it is almost more than the mind can compass." With the freedom that the Church has always allowed to her children in their spiritual life, Teilhard dispensed with certain features that in his view were too personal, too restrictive, though retained by the devotion of recent centuries; at the same time, it was, indeed, as he says, "under the sign of, and filled with wonder by, the Heart of Jesus," that his religious life developed. "To what depths, with what vigour and continuity" it would be difficult, he adds, to explain. More and more, for Teilhard, the Heart of Jesus was the "Fire," bursting into the cosmic milieu, to "amorize" it. He always carried a picture of the Sacred Heart in his breviary, a link between the invocations he had been taught and those which he now found better nourishment for his prayer. He turned his eyes toward its rays, carrying radiance to all parts [of the universe]. . . . Thus the concept, which was so dear to him and that in the end was supreme

in him, of the "universal Christ" was born from "an expansion of the Heart of Jesus." (De Lubac, pp. 46–47)

So much a part of his spirituality was his devotion to the Sacred Heart that Teilhard scarcely needed to be reminded of the commission given much later to each Jesuit:

> All should have a high regard for, and be keenly mindful of, the mystery of the Heart of Christ in the life of the Church. It should be so much a part of their own lives that they can promote it among others in their every apostolic activity, as a most pleasant responsibility entrusted to the Society [of Jesus] by Christ our Lord. In this way the results of our varied ministries may daily increase. (Padberg, p. 301)

Pause: Make time to reflect on ways in which Jesus has shown love for you and ways in which you have returned that love or ways in which you hope to return that love.

Teilhard's Words

In his book *Teilhard de Chardin and the Mystery of Christ*, Christopher Mooney notes that Teilhard held a heartfelt conviction that human achievement would "in some sense be eternalized and saved" (p. 22). He points out that this conviction was more the result of an early-in-life "attraction for the absolute deeply imbedded in his personality" (p. 22). Teilhard called this attraction at various times a "cosmic sense," a "sense of plenitude," a "human sense," "a sense of fulfillment." "Now *pari passu* with the evolution in me of this innate cosmic sense. . . . another process begun by education, never ceased to follow its course in my mind and heart: I mean the awakening of a certain Christic sense" (p. 22). Teilhard explains how at last he grasped the connection, the convergence, and finally the identity of these two axes that served as the source and motivation for much of his theological writing:

> The movement which drew me into its current based itself upon a point, upon a person, myself. . . . But very

soon I found this same self of mine caught up in another direction. Along with everything around me I experienced a sense of being seized by a movement of a higher order, which shuffled all the elements of my universe and re-grouped them in a new sequence. And when it was given me to see where this dazzling trail was leading, . . . I discovered that everything was again centered upon a Point, upon a Person, and this Person was you, Jesus! . . . From the moment that you said "This is my Body," not only the bread on the altar, but to a certain extent everything in the universe became yours that nourishes in our souls the life of grace and the spirit. (Mooney, p. 23)

Many people, especially during his lifetime, considered Teilhard so avant-garde as to be dangerous. The truth is that at core he was quite traditional. He found in Saint Paul one whose heart was ablaze with love for Jesus, a kindred spirit who spoke and wrote boldly about the fire of love that prodded him on. Teilhard said of himself that he wished to unite "the spirit of tradition and the spirit of adventurous research" (De Lubac, p. 4).

Reflection

Pope Leo XIII in his encyclical *Annum Sacrum* (Holy Year), recognizing the many wounds from which society was suffering, and especially "the rapidly spreading disbelief in the supernatural," consecrated the whole human race to the Sacred Heart of Jesus "who is the heir of all things" (Hebrews 1:2). The worship of the Sacred Heart is essentially the same as that which we give to the Body of Christ because it concerns the same person. Moreover, it focuses on the heart as the symbol of the love of the incarnate Word made manifest in the central life-giving mysteries of the Incarnation and Redemption. Thus in reality this devotion is as old as Christianity because it focuses on Christ's humanity. Only the emphasis is different because its prime goal is to make clear the message that Jesus' life from the manger to the Resurrection was an uninterrupted manifestation of God's love.

✧ Examine the text of 1 John 4:8,16. Repeat the words "God is love" over and over.

✧ Reread 1 John 4:16. Reflect on God's love, which is a very special kind of love—*agape* is the Greek word that has been chosen by John. Agapic love is a love that is selfless—it means self-gift. It is not *eros*, which is a love that seeks fulfillment in that which is loved—the word *erotic* comes from *eros*. It is not *philia*, which is companionable love or friendship. *Agape* is love that is entirely directed toward another, a kind of love that seeks no response and demands no return, a love that is focused totally on the beloved. Reflect on the kinds of love you have known. Who has shown you agapic love? To whom have you given this special kind of love?

✧ *Agape* can be translated as self-gift. This is the gift of oneself to the other without any regard to whether the gift is accepted or returned. When a firefighter or a mother dashes into a burning building to rescue a trapped child, that is *agape*, or agapic love. It is the kind of love that Jesus was referring to when he said, "Greater love than this no one has than that they lay down their life for a friend." Isn't that all the more true if one lays down one's life for a person who is not yet a friend? Think of a situation where you might show agapic love to someone who is not a friend or family member.

✧ Read this prayer with all the sincerity that you feel:

O God, what will you do to conquer
the fearful hardness of our hearts?

. . . .

You must give us your own Heart, Jesus

. . . .

Place your Heart deep in the center of our hearts
and enkindle in each heart a flame of love
as strong, as great, as the sum of all the reasons
that I have for loving you, my God.

(Colombiere, p. 54)

God's Word

The devotion to the Sacred Heart of Jesus was unknown as such to writers of the Old Testament and New Testament. The spirit of the devotion to the Sacred Heart, however, was well known to numerous Scripture writers because it emphasized God's great love for human beings, compassion for the human condition, and God as our help in all ages.

Major aspects of Teilhard's spirituality and thought were firmly grounded in the devotion to the Sacred Heart. Teilhard in *The Heart of Matter* alludes to certain moving biblical scenes such as Moses and the burning bush on the mountain. He suggests a transposition into a modern perspective for the Christian who on a journey through the burning desert after fleeing from slavery discovers blazing images and pillars of fire that illuminate our relationship with God and the universe.

We stand barefoot on holy ground as we worship with Teilhard in the light of the luminous flames rising from the Sacred Heart of Jesus; the cosmic Christ; Christ, the evolver; the ever greater Christ. The following Scripture passage written by Saint Paul is read on the feast of the Sacred Heart. It is one of the many Pauline texts that inspired Teilhard as he offered this Mass. This passage expresses the unconditional love that Jesus has for his pilgrim people. Saint Paul speaks lyrically in many places about the extravagant love that Jesus has for all of us humans, as, for example, in chapter 3, his letter to the Ephesians:

> I kneel before the Father, from whom every family in heaven and on earth is named, that he may grant you in accord with the riches of his glory to be strengthened with power through his Spirit in the inner self, and that Christ may dwell in your hearts through faith; that you, rooted and grounded in love, may have strength to comprehend with all the holy ones what is the breadth and length and height and depth, and to know the love of Christ that surpasses all knowledge, so that you may be filled with all the fullness of God. (Vv. 14–19)

Closing prayer:

> Lord of consistence and union, you whose *distinguishing mark* . . . is the power indefinitely to grow greater, without distortion or loss of continuity, to the measure of the mysterious Matter whose Heart you fill and all whose movements you ultimately control—Lord of my childhood and Lord of my last days—God complete in relation to yourself and yet, for us, continually being born—God, who, because you offer yourself to our worship as "evolver" and "evolving," are henceforth the only being that can satisfy us—sweep away the last clouds that still hide you—the clouds of hostile prejudice and those, too, of false creeds. (King, *Spirit of Fire,* p. 204)

Jesus, the Cosmic Christ

Theme: Jesus is the center toward which all things are moving!

Opening prayer: "Lord Jesus, you are the center toward which all things are moving: . . . make a place for us all in the company of those elect and holy ones whom your loving care has liberated one by one from the chaos of our present existence and who now are being slowly incorporated into you in the unity of the new earth" (*Hymn of the Universe*, p. 74).

About Teilhard

The Armistice was signed in November 1918, and Teilhard was mustered out of the service of the military on 10 March 1919. During the more than four years that he was mainly at the front, he had firsthand experience of the human destruction war caused. Ten million had died, killed violently on the battlefields, in unimaginable horror. Teilhard expressed eloquently his nostalgia for the front in an essay that expresses a profound biblical mysticism reminiscent of the glorious creation of the New Jerusalem of the Book of Revelation (chapters 21–22):

> It is true to say that without this new and superhuman soul which takes over from our own at the Front, there

would be things to endure and see up there that would be intolerable. . . .

 For my own part I can say that without war there would be a world of feelings that I would never otherwise have known or suspected. . . . When the air of Flanders stank of chlorine . . . when [the charred hillsides] . . . held the odour of death . . . And as I turned to take a last look at that . . . living line of the Front, it was then that in the flash of a nascent intuition I half-saw that the line was taking on the shape of a higher Thing, of great nobility, which I could feel was forming itself even as I watched. (*Heart of Matter,* pp. 178–179)

Back in Paris by 1919, Teilhard set about passing his several certificates in geology, botany, and zoology. In 1922 he was conferred the title of doctor, with distinction.

It seems that many of us mortals are commonly attracted to think of ways in which we may be immortalized. Different avenues of human achievement may offer themselves as paths to fulfilling our deep conviction, as it was Teilhard's also, that our human achievement will "in some sense be eternalized and saved." This seems to be what his childhood attraction for the Absolute was all about, a sense or instinct that was deeply embedded in his personality. Teilhard called this attraction by various names, including "a cosmic sense." At the same time, we may be attracted by a "Christic sense" as Teilhard was, namely an attraction to a love of God. Teilhard thought of these two attractions, as I have elaborated in an earlier meditation, as "two axes apparently independent of each other at birth; yet only after much time and effort did I grasp . . . their connection, their convergence and finally their ultimate identity" (Mooney, pp. 22–23).

 The personal and intellectual synthesis to which Teilhard devoted his life focused on a search for an explanation of his conviction that Christ's physical relationship to the universe as a whole was through humankind. His preoccupation was to discover unity between God and the world. His background as a geologist, whose primary specialty was mammalian paleontology, early furnished him with evidence for evolution in his study of life forms in rocks of the last sixty-five million years. This in turn led him to think of God as the Great Evolver. On the other hand he saw in the writings of Saint Paul and Saint John intimations of evolution in terms of human contributions to the development of the Kingdom of Christ on Earth. It seems certain that Paul recognized some kind of physical relationship between Christ and the members of his Body-Person. It seems probable from the context that this relationship was extended through humankind to the whole of creation.

Pause: Try to realize that your God and savior is also Creator of the entire cosmos and loves you personally.

Teilhard's Words

The "Pensees," short selections of which are used below, consist of eighty-one short poetic selections from a great variety of Teilhard's published and unpublished works. I believe they will help to prepare you for meditation.

> Since Jesus was born, and grew to his full stature, and died, everything has continued to move forward *because Christ is not yet fully formed:* he has not yet gathered about him the last folds of his robe of flesh and of love which is made up of his faithful followers. The mystical Christ has not yet attained to his full growth; and therefore the same is true of the cosmic Christ. Both of these are simultaneously in the state of being and of becoming; and it is from the prolongation of this process of becoming that all created activity ultimately springs. Christ is the end point of the evolution, even the *natural* evolution, of all beings; and therefore evolution is holy. (*Hymn of the Universe,* p. 137)

The concept of the cosmic Christ brings to mind the limitless expanse of the physical universe. The vast period of some twelve billion years since the universe was created, and the nearly five billion years that have gone by since the Earth coalesced from rocky galactic dust and then evolved to its present form, helps us to imagine the vast reaches of time and constant change as we look back toward the beginning:

The prodigious expanses of time which preceded the first Christmas were not empty of Christ: they were imbued with the influx of his power. It was the ferment of his conception that stirred up the cosmic masses and directed the initial developments of the biosphere. It was the travail preceding his birth that accelerated the development of instinct and the birth of thought upon the earth. . . . All these preparatory processes were cosmically and biologically [and, I (James W. Skehan, SJ) must add, physically] necessary that Christ might set foot upon our human stage. And all this labor was set in motion by the active, creative awakening of his soul inasmuch as that human soul had been chosen to breathe life into the universe. When Christ first appeared before [us] in the arms of Mary he had already stirred up the world. (*Hymn of the Universe,* pp. 74–75)

In discussing the cosmic sense and the Christic sense, Teilhard addresses the tension, which at times may become ambivalence, the either-or question of how to live a life of human achievement or to withdraw into total seclusion in the monastery of our own heart. The real question for so many of us is how we can combine the two axes of our life as lived, the question that Teilhard addresses in the following:

Even when it has become clear to all that religious faith is not hostile to progress but represents, rather, an additional force to be used by Christians [and I, J. W. S., would add by all religious persons], in the name of what they hold most sacred, to forward the common task of evolution, even then, I fear, we shall not have complete harmony between the children of Heaven and the sons of earth. Too many will still prefer to run away from the Gospel and worship the Golden Calf or look in the sky for some star other than Christ. The Parousia, we know, is promised as a dawn that will rise over a supreme onslaught of error. . . . Yet, wise with the experience of centuries, she [the church] will be able proudly to point out . . . her finest children busy in *forwarding, side by side, mastery of the world and the Kingdom of God.* (*Writings in Time of War,* p. 91)

Reflection

✧ Do you recognize in yourself an attraction for the Absolute deeply imbedded in your personality as Teilhard did—a cosmic sense? At the same time has there awakened in you a certain Christic sense? Have the two axes of your life, cosmic sense and the Christic sense, become ultimately identical in some way or centered on a point, that point being the person of Christ?

✧ Teilhard helps you to reflect on the two axes of your life, your activity and your need to adore:

> God, at his most vitally active and most incarnate, is not remote from us, wholly apart from the sphere of the tangible; on the contrary, at every moment he awaits us in the activity, the work to be done, which every moment brings. He is, in a sense, at the point of my pen, my pick, my paint brush, my needle—and my heart and my thought. It is by carrying to its natural completion the stroke, the line, the stitch I am working on that I shall lay hold on that ultimate end toward which my will at its deepest levels tends. . . . [T]he enormous might of God's magnetism is brought to bear on our frail desires, our tiny objectives. . . . It endues us with supervitality, and therefore introduces into our spiritual life a higher principle of unity, the specific effect of which can be seen—according to one's point of view—as either to make human endeavor holy or to make the Christian life fully human. (*Hymn of the Universe,* pp. 82–83)

God's Word

The following are two so-called cosmic texts or key passages in Saint Paul's letters that are commonly offered as a response to the question asked by Mooney, "To what extent can Paul be said to extend the physical relationship between Christ and mankind to the whole of creation, including therefore all that is material?" (p. 94). An important text to be considered is from Romans 8:19–23:

> For creation is waiting with eager longing for the revelation of the sons of God: if it has been condemned to frustration—not through its own fault but because of him who so condemned it,—it also has hope of being set free in its turn from the bondage of decay and of entering into the freedom of the glory of the children of God. We know indeed that the whole of creation has been groaning until now in an agony of birth. More than that, we ourselves who already possess in the Spirit a foretaste of the future, groan also in our hearts, waiting for the redemption of our bodies. (As quoted in Mooney, p. 95)
>
> What is important for us here is first of all Paul's insistence that it is the *whole* of creation, man therefore included, which is the object of redemption, and secondly that it is precisely through the bodies of men that redemption extends to the rest of creation. (P. 95)

The restoration of the universe in Christ became Paul's dominant preoccupation in writing to the Colossians and Ephesians. He returns to Christ's pre-existence with the Father,

> in whose image he is the source as well as the instrument and final end of creation. The Incarnation, crowned by the triumph of the Resurrection, is seen as placing the human nature of Christ at the head not only of the whole human race but also of the entire created universe, the latter indirectly concerned in the salvation of man as it had been in his fall. . . .
>
> For many exegetes today the "Plenitude" of Christ in this extraordinary text, his Pleroma, represents in Paul's mind the extension of Christ's redemption to the whole cosmos, the whole of creation. . . . In Colossians and Ephesians Paul strips it of its stoic pantheism and gives it a content familiar to the Old Testament, that of the cosmos filled with the creative presence of God. The "fullness"

which resides in Christ, therefore, is "the plenitude of being," including both the fullness of divinity and the fullness of the universe. Christ is God, and through his work of redemption he unites to himself not only redeemed humanity, for which Paul reserves the term "Body," but also the whole of the cosmos which is humanity's dwelling place. (Pp. 96–97)

Ephesians 1:9–10,22–23 contains a major development in Paul's thought inasmuch as God's plan of salvation is described as a "re-establishment" or a "summing up" of all things in Christ.

It is quite possible from the context that Paul's intention here is to situate squarely within a cosmic framework his Body-of-Christ theme, and at the same time to present the relationship between Christ and the cosmos as an extension of the physical and sacramental relationship between Christ and the members of his Church. Not only is Christ Lord of the universe, he is also its "Head." This hypothesis seems to be confirmed by the verses that follow, in which the Church, as the risen Body of Christ, becomes extended . . . and equated with the dimensions of the Pleroma, "the Plenitude of him who is everywhere and in all things complete." Moreover, the "fullness of time" in which this Plenitude is to be realized refers most probably to *both* comings of Christ, his Incarnation and work of Redemption in time and his *Parousia* at the end of time. Thus, in Ephesians 3:19 the Plenitude is seen to be ultimately the Plenitude of God, into which the love of Christ will eventually bring both cosmos and Church in the final and definitive achievement of cosmic as well as salvation history." (Mooney, pp. 98–99).

Closing prayer: "You the Centre at which all things meet and which stretches out over all things so as to draw them back into itself: I love you for the extensions of your body and soul to the furthest corners of creation through grace, through life, and through matter" (*Writings in Time of War*, p. 70).

✧ Meditation 13 ✧

The Body of Christ

Theme: "The mystical Christ, the universal Christ of St. Paul, has neither meaning nor value in our eyes except as an expansion of the Christ who was born of Mary and who died on the Cross. . . . However far we may be drawn into the divine spaces opened up to us by Christian mysticism, we never depart from the Jesus of the Gospels" (*Divine Milieu*, p. 117).

Opening prayer:

Lord Jesus, carrying farther the process of your Incarnation, you come down into the bread and live there, your presence is not confined to that particle of matter. The transubstantiation is encircled by a halo of divinisation— real, even though less intense—that extends to the whole universe. . . . I shall look beyond the white host, accepting its domination, and with all the strength of my desire and my prayer, with all my power, over every substance and every development, I shall pronounce the words: This is my Body! (Based on *Writings in Time of War*, p. 207)

About Teilhard

Teilhard's orientation as a Jesuit geologist was to investigate the earth and the universe by means of scientific methods and to examine whatever paradigms and theories from science might help to illuminate the relationship between science and religion. Teilhard was intensely interested in the writings of Saint Paul in which he recognized the possibility of expanding theological insights related to creation. He was especially interested in the implications of the Incarnation and of the Mystical Body of Christ to the created universe. Teilhard picked up on the Body of Christ theme in Saint Paul and applied it to understanding possible relationships with Christ throughout the universe and especially to concepts of Christogenesis and cosmogenesis.

> "Let us return to Paul," said Teilhard in a 1930 lecture. "Let us remember that the supernatural nourishes itself on everything, and let us accept fully those magnificent perspectives according to which the Christ of St. Paul appears to us as he in whom all has been created and he in whom the whole world finds its stability, with all its height and depth, its grandeur and greatness, with all that is material and all that is spiritual." This in turn means seeing everything "from the point of view of the organization of the Pleroma (which is the only true point of view from which the world can be understood)." (Mooney, p. 100)

For Teilhard Christ is always the person, Jesus, the Christ of the Gospels. In other words, for Teilhard the Mystical Body of Christ must be thought of as a physical reality:

> At the time of the First World War . . . , when thinking about the mystery of the "body of Christ," which includes the mystery of the "communion of Saints" and which is "bound up in the blessed unity of a physically organized whole," he was filled with wonder at its "so astonishingly cosmic character." Then he offered himself to God, meditating . . . on his priesthood in order (as he said in his prayer) that "in my own humble way I may be the apostle and . . . the evangelist of your Christ in the universe." . . . It was simply that his own spontaneous urge, matured by an inner vision, reinforced and enriched by all his reflection, fostered, too, by the developments of his scientific thought, was leading him towards Him

whom he called the "universal Christ." (De Lubac, pp. 30–31)

Pause: Reflect, as Teilhard did, on the personal meaning for you of the Body of Christ that includes all your loved ones, living and dead.

Teilhard's Words

Teilhard was concerned with the successful outcome of human work, human effort and suffering. As a result he was fascinated by Saint Paul's concept of the Pleroma. Teilhard refers to the consummation of the world as the communion of saints; Saint Paul calls it the Pleroma, meaning a fulfillment of the divine plan of salvation, the "completing" of the world. Teilhard was interested in how the individual person might contribute to this fulfillment of that plan.

> What is the supreme and complex reality for which the divine operation moulds us? It is revealed to us by St. Paul and St. John. It is the quantitative repletion and the qualitative consummation of all things: it is the mysterious Pleroma, in which the substantial *one* and the created *many* fuse without confusion in a *whole* which, without adding anything essential to God, will nevertheless be a sort of triumph and generalisation of being. . . .
> . . . What is the active centre, the living link, the organising soul of the Pleroma? St. Paul, again, proclaims it with all his resounding voice: it is he in whom everything is reunited, and in whom all things are consummated—through whom the whole created edifice receives its consistency—Christ dead and risen [who fills up everything, in whom everything has its being].
> . . . The divine omnipresence translates itself within our universe by the network of the organising forces of the total Christ. . . . In it [the divine milieu] we recognise an omnipresence which acts upon us by assimilating us in it, [in the unity of the Body of Christ]. As a consequence of the Incarnation, the divine immensity has

transformed itself for us into *the omnipresence of christifica-tion*. All the good that I can do . . . is physically gathered in, by something of itself, into the reality of the consummated Christ. Everything I endure, with faith and love, by way of diminishment or death, makes me a little more closely an integral part of his mystical body. Quite specifically it is *Christ whom we make or whom we undergo in all things*. Not only [for those who love, everything is transformed into good] but, more clearly still, [they are transformed in God] and quite explicitly [they are transformed in Christ].

. . . The human layer of the earth is wholly and continuously under the organising influx of the incarnate Christ. (*Divine Milieu*, pp. 122–124)

Reflection

Teilhard was preoccupied with the question of whether human activity was worth anything in the long run—does what I do matter? Teilhard was convinced that our efforts are important and that our works have an everlasting value that will never be lost. The "Teilhard's Words" section above implies that not only is the work that we do worthwhile but that Christ stimulates in us a desire to collaborate with others in the human effort in which we are engaged.

✧ As is usual with Teilhard, the word *collaborate* has overtones from the meditations on the passion and death of Jesus in *The Spiritual Exercises* of Saint Ignatius, in which Teilhard was steeped. Meditate on how Jesus labors and suffers for you and reflect on what you are willing to endure in collaborating with those who labor in Christ's vineyard.

God's Word

Paul is speaking of the attitude of reverence that the Corinthians should have as they assemble for the celebration of the remembrance of the Lord's Supper, the eucharistic meal.

As a body is one though it has many parts, and all the parts of the body, though many, are one body, so also Christ. For in one Spirit we were all baptized into one body, whether Jews or Greeks, slaves or free persons, and we were all given to drink of one Spirit.

   . . . But as it is, there are many parts, yet one body. . . . If [one] part suffers, all the parts suffer with it; if one part is honored, all the parts share its joy. (1 Corinthians 12:12–27)

Closing prayer: God, creator of the universe, what marvelous blessings you have showered on me and on the universe in the Incarnation of Jesus, your divine Word made flesh. You nourish my spirit with the elements of Jesus' own life, his body and blood. You nourish my mind and heart with knowledge of your created universe and how it works. I thank you, Jesus, for the gift of Teilhard's insights into my own personal participation in Jesus' Incarnation and Resurrection, through the Eucharist and the assurance that I have a role to play in bringing to completion the Pleroma, because Jesus has given me a share in the fullness of divinity, and new life in company with Christ.

✦　**Meditation 14**　✦

Progress of the World

Theme: Humankind contributes not only to the progress of the world but also the completion of Christ.

Opening prayer: God, our Creator, give me sight, give me insight that I may learn to view all of your creation, all of your creatures as you see them. At creation you loved them into being, and you saw that they were good! Jesus, my brother, may I lose my fear of change and human progress however threatening I may perceive it to be. Enlighten the minds and soften the hearts of all members of your human family that we may be patient in setbacks, forgiving of human sinfulness even as you are, diligent in encouraging those who need our help to live more unselfishly, and earnestly prayerful in reaching out to the whole world. Help us live in the dignity that befits humans because we share the same humanity as you, our savior, Jesus Christ!

About Teilhard

Teilhard had an optimistic outlook on life and the prospect that the work of Christ in the world would turn out successfully in spite of the obviously sinful and even depraved state of affairs in the world. His optimism was born of a deep-rooted faith in the efficacy of the Incarnation in the lives, sufferings, deaths, and resurrection of those who share their humanity with Jesus.

A magnificent concept developed by Teilhard is that of *Christogenesis,* the universe becoming Christ, we might say, which he describes concretely: "When our action is animated by grace . . . it builds up a true Body, that of Christ, who wished to be completed through each one of us" (Mooney, pp. 148–149). Teilhard attempts to explain how there can be a Christogenesis, and how in the long run it is possible to speak of the two movements of Christogenesis and cosmogenesis, ongoing creation, as one and the same. Basically Teilhard's concept of creation is viewed as a "temporal Christogenesis moving towards the final Plenitude of Christ" (Mooney, p. 148).

Teilhard noted that Christ's Body is a physical reality inserted into humanity through the Incarnation as well as into an evolving universe. As a result of the physical incompleteness of the Body of Christ, we can bring Christ to completion in some way.

From this line of thought, Teilhard develops what will become over the next ten years of his life a preoccupation with the cosmic Christ as well as what he believed to be a valid Christian outlook on the world: Because "the cosmos is centred upon Jesus, it should be clear that in one way or another collaboration in the future of the cosmos is an essential and primary part of Christian responsibility. Nature grows towards fulfillment and the Body of Christ reaches its complete development in one and the same movement" (p. 149). Teilhard asks the question that forms a central theme in *The Divine Milieu:* "Who will be the Christian . . . to make every drop of sap from the world flow into his own movement towards the divine Trinity? It will be he who has understood that to be fully a child of God, to accomplish fully his holy will, one must show oneself more diligent in earthly work than any servant of Mammon" (Mooney, p. 150).

Pause: Gaze in joy and wonder at your privilege of participating in the universe becoming Christ and in ongoing creation.

Teilhard's Words

The question of when and how the end times may come may be of little interest to each of us as individuals unless we happen to think that the end of the world is imminent. The important thing is our personal relationship to Christ in our daily life and that we personally expect to encounter Christ in the world of our everyday life.

> We are sometimes inclined to think that the same things are monotonously repeated over and over again in the history of creation. That is because the season is too long by comparison with the brevity of our individual lives, and the transformation too vast and too inward by comparison with our superficial and restricted outlook, for us to see the progress of what is tirelessly taking place in and through all matter and all spirit. Let us believe in revelation, once again our faithful support in our most human forebodings. Under the commonplace envelope of things . . . a new earth is being slowly engendered.
>
> One day, the Gospel tells us, the tension gradually accumulating between humanity and God will touch the limits prescribed by the possibilities of the world. . . . Then will come the end. Then the presence of Christ, which has been silently accruing in things, will suddenly be revealed—like a flash of light from pole to pole. . . . The spiritual atoms of the world . . . will occupy, . . . (always under the influence of Christ) the place of happiness or pain designated for them by the living structure of the Pleroma. . . . Like lightning, like a conflagration, like a flood, the attraction exerted by the Son of Man will lay hold of all the whirling elements in the universe so as to reunite them or subject them to his body. . . .
>
> Such will be the consummation of the divine *milieu.* (*Divine Milieu*, pp. 150–151)

In the final paragraphs of *The Divine Milieu,* Teilhard starts to chide pessimistic or fearful men and women in the words Jesus used when he reached out his hand and caught Peter as he was sinking after so bravely walking out to meet

Jesus by walking on the water, "O you of little faith, why do you doubt?"

> Men of little faith, why then do you fear or repudiate the progress of the world? Why foolishly multiply your warnings and your prohibitions? "Don't venture . . . Don't try . . . everything is known: the earth is empty and old: there is nothing more to be discovered."
> We must try everything for Christ; we must hope everything for Christ. [Leave nothing untried!] That, on the contrary, is the true christian attitude. To divinise does not mean to destroy, but to sur-create. We shall never know all that the Incarnation still expects of the world's potentialities. We shall never put enough hope in the growing unity of mankind. (P. 154)

In a final burst of exuberance, Teilhard addresses the city that Jesus loved, the city seated on the mountain from which God's Word goes out to those of many faiths, the city that put him to the death from which he rose gloriously as the promise of a successful outcome for each one of us:

> Jerusalem, lift up your head. Look at the immense crowds of those who build and those who seek. All over the world, men are toiling—in laboratories, in studios, in deserts, in factories, in the vast social crucible. The ferment that is taking place by their instrumentality in art and science and thought is happening for your sake. Open, then, your arms and your heart, like Christ your Lord, and welcome the waters, the flood and the sap of humanity. Accept it, this sap—for, without its baptism, you will wither, without desire, like a flower out of water; and tend it, since, without your sun, it will disperse itself wildly in sterile shoots. (P. 154).

And finally Teilhard concludes almost rapturously:

> Now the earth can certainly clasp me in her giant arms. She can swell me with her life, or take me back into her dust. She can deck herself out for me with every charm, with every horror, with every mystery. She can intoxicate me with her perfume of tangibility and unity. She can cast

me to my knees in expectation of what is maturing in her breast. . . .

But her enchantments can no longer do me harm, since she has become for me, over and above herself, the body of him who is and of him who is coming.

The divine milieu. (Pp. 154–155)

Reflection

✧ Do you find it inspiring to recall the sincerity that was shown by Old Testament figures such as Anna and Simeon who came to the Temple each day to devoutly pray for the coming of the Messiah? If Jesus had not yet come into the world, would you be more inclined than you are to pray earnestly that God's influence might be magnified in the world through your efforts?

✧ Reflect, as Teilhard did, that creation was not finished long ago, but that we can serve to complete creation with whatever activity in which we become involved, and so help to build the Pleroma, that is to help complete creation. Make your own those encouraging words of Teilhard: "In action I adhere to the creative power of God; I become not only its instrument but its living extension" (Mooney, p. 152).

God's Word

Matthew presents a very moving scene from the *Parousia*:

When the Son of Man comes in his glory, and all the angels with him, he will sit upon his glorious throne, and all the nations will be assembled before him. And he will separate them one from another, as a shepherd separates the sheep from the goats. He will place the sheep on his right and the goats on his left. Then the king will say to those on his right, "Come, you who are blessed by my Father. Inherit the kingdom prepared for you from the foundation of the world. For I was hungry and you gave me food, I was thirsty and you gave me drink, a stranger and you welcomed me, naked and you clothed me, ill and you cared for me, in prison and you visited me." Then the righteous will answer him and say, "Lord, when did we see you hungry and feed you, or thirsty and give you drink? When did we see you a stranger and welcome you, or naked and clothe you? When did we see you ill or in prison, and visit you?" And the king will say to them in reply, "Amen, I say to you, whatever you did for one of these least brothers of mine, you did for me." (Matthew 25:31–40).

Closing: I am grateful to you, O Lord, that in your divine providence you have given me an opportunity to share in your Incarnation as a member of the human race. I thank you for your gift of life as well as for setting me on a path by which I have come to know and love you, a path that has led me to understand that by means of the talents and work that you have placed in my hands, not only can I contribute to the progress of humankind but especially that I, as cocreator and coredeemer with you, can bring you to completion in some way.

✧ Meditation 15 ✧

Immersed in God and the World

Theme: Our time on Earth is an opportunity to immerse ourselves in the atmosphere of God's nourishing life and love while working with our endowments of nature and nurture so that we may with God build the Earth in a way that will give the most meaning for us and for all those who can be uplifted by our labors.

Opening prayer: Lord Jesus, because you created the universe and the Earth, I picture you as a working God. All that I have and all of the opportunities that come my way are due to the work of those who have nurtured me.

About Teilhard

Teilhard, as a Jesuit, was intimately familiar with the spiritual exercises of Saint Ignatius. Although he did not commonly refer to them explicitly, the themes and treatment of the spiritual exercises run throughout Teilhard's writings, most notably his Christ-focused and Trinity-focused writings. Ignatius was a mystic who was action oriented, portraying Jesus as an attractive leader and collaborator with whom we can develop a close personal relationship.

Although the principle and foundation of the Ignatian exercises are an important beginning for founding a solid spirituality, they are only that. Teilhard goes much farther in all of his writings because he is consumed with the intensity of his friendship with Jesus and his role as collaborator, cocreator and coredeemer with him. The overpowering intensity of his drive to write and publish his voluminous geologic research and spirituality research is a clue to his intense relationship with Jesus and with his ever-widening circle of friends.

Teilhard and his lifelong project can be best understood by taking him at face value—a devout, intense person with a brilliant mind who was enthralled both by the beauty of the world around him, by the God whose creation it was in the last analysis, and by the incarnate Christ, the Word of God and son of Mary. He was consumed by a desire to explore as fully as possible and to develop religious insights from Scripture embellished by insights growing out of his scientific experience.

Pause: Imagine yourself situated in any part of Earth or the universe that most inspires you and reflect that you are indeed totally immersed in the atmosphere of God's nourishing life and love.

Teilhard's Words

In writing about the eternal value, or divinization, of our activities Teilhard refers to them as the "stones of which is built the New Jerusalem" (*Divine Milieu*, p. 54), a symbol that inspired Teilhard and one that had inspired the people of Israel who, during their fifty years of captivity in Babylon, longed to return to the New Jerusalem, the mountain of God.

He says as a partial answer to the question of the value of human action: "But what *will* count, up there, what *will* always endure, is this: that you have acted in all things *conformably* to the will of God" (p. 54). Teilhard goes further, suggesting passionately that an essential ingredient must be a sense of "achievement which our spiritual peace and joy so imperiously demand" (p. 55).

Teilhard is clearly concerned with the activity of the individual person but throughout his life he was intensely interested in unity and cooperation among the peoples of the world, and the value of group effort. He addresses a basic proposal to the Christian:

> To what power is it reserved to burst asunder the envelopes in which our individual microcosms tend jealously to isolate themselves and to vegetate? To what force is it given to merge and exalt our partial rays into the principal radiance of Christ? To charity, the source and consequence of every spiritual relationship. "Christian charity, preached with such solemnity by the Gospel, is nothing else than the more or less conscious cohesion of souls engendered by their communal convergence *in Christo Jesu*. It is impossible to love Christ without loving others; . . . and it is impossible to love others . . . without in one and the same movement coming closer to Christ. Automatically, therefore, by a sort of living determinism, the individual divine milieu . . . tend to fuse one with another. . . . The only subject ultimately capable of spiritual transfiguration is the totality of men forming together a single body and a single soul in charity.
> . . . Charity no longer demands that we merely bind up wounds; it urges us to build a better world here on earth and to be in the first ranks of every campaign for the full development of mankind. (Mooney, pp. 152–153)

God's Word

Teilhard's starting point in dealing with his theory of "creative union" is what has been revealed about Christ's relationship to all of creation from the beginning of time. Teilhard emphasizes the importance of Colossians 1:15–17, a part of Paul's letter devoted to the pre-eminence of Christ:

> He is the image of the invisible God,
>   The firstborn of all creation.
> For in him were created all things in heaven and on earth,
>   The visible and the invisible,

Whether thrones or dominions or principalities or
    powers;
All things were created through him and for him.
He is before all things,
    And in him all things hold together.

(Col. 1:15–17)

For us there is one
God, the Father,
    from whom all things are and for whom we exist,
and one Lord, Jesus Christ,
    through whom all things are and through whom we
    exist.

(1 Corinthians 8:6)

Reflection

During his long recovery from a near-fatal wound as a soldier in battle, Ignatius of Loyola, a less-than-devout Catholic in his twenties at the time, developed a methodology for discovering what in his lifestyle and decision making led to true peace and what left him discontented. Over a long period of conversion, he wrote down his observations and these became the little book *The Spiritual Exercises*. One of Ignatius's foundational ideas for sound decision making was what he called the principle and foundation:

> Man is created to praise, reverence, and serve God our Lord, and by this means to save his soul.
>
> And the other things on the face of the earth are created for man and that they may help in prosecuting the end for which he is created.
>
> From this it follows that man is to use them as much as they help him on to his end, and ought to rid himself of them so far as they hinder him as to it.
>
> For this it is necessary to make ourselves indifferent to all created things in all that is allowed to the choice of our free will and is not prohibited to it; so that, on our part, we want not health rather than sickness, riches rather than poverty, honor rather than dishonor, long rather

than short life, and so in all the rest; desiring and choosing only what is most conducive for us to the end for which we are created. (Fleming, p. 26)

✧ Think of a decision you need to make. What would lead you to true peace? To discontentment?

✧ In reckless generosity ask yourself: "What have I done for Christ? What am I doing for Christ? What will I do for Christ?" In Teilhard's writings we see him filled with the fire of intense desire to do great things for the greater glory of God, for the ever greater Christ.

Closing prayer: Lord, throughout all ages you have been our rock and our salvation. You still walk the road to Emmaus, seeking those who may recognize you in the breaking of the bread, seeking out those who want to be healed. Give sight and insight to me and my beloved companions on the journey that, while we love the cosmic world, we may ever find you at its center, Lord. May your sacred name be ever in my heart and on my lips!

J·E·S·U·S

✧ Works Cited ✧

Appleton-Weber, Sarah, ed. and trans. *The Human Phenomenon.* Brighton, England: Sussex Academic Press, 1999.

Barbour, George B. *In the Field with Teilhard de Chardin.* New York: Herder and Herder, 1965.

Bergant, Dianne, CSA, and Robert J. Karris, OFM. *The Collegeville Bible Commentary.* Collegeville, MN: Liturgical Press, 1989.

Buckley, Cornelius Michael, SJ, ed. and trans. *Ignatius of Loyola: The Pilgrim Saint.* Chicago: Loyola University Press, 1994.

Cuenot, Claude. *Teilhard de Chardin: A Bibliographic Study.* Baltimore, MD: Helicon Press, 1965.

De Lubac, Henri, SJ. *Teilhard de Chardin: The Man and His Meaning.* New York: Hawthorn Books, 1965.

Egan, Harvey D., SJ. *What Are they Saying About Mysticism?* Ramsey, NJ: Paulist Press, 1982.

Fleming, David L., SJ. *Draw Me into Your Friendship: The Spiritual Exercises.* Saint Louis: Institute of Jesuit Sources, 1996.

Himes, Michael. "Living Conversations: Higher Education in a Catholic Context." *Conversations on Jesuit Higher Education.* No. 8, Fall 1995.

Johnson, Elizabeth. "Mary of Nazareth: Friend of God and Prophet." *America.* 17–24 June 2000.

King, Thomas, *Teilhard de Chardin, The Way of the Christian Mystics.* Vol. 6. Wilmington, DE: Michael Glazier, 1988.

———. *Teilhard's Mysticism of Knowing.* New York: Seabury Press, 1981.

King, Thomas M., SJ, and Mary Wood Gilbert. *The Letters of Teilhard de Chardin and Lucille Swan.* Washington, D.C.: Georgetown University Press, 1993.

King, Ursula. *Christ in All Things: Exploring Spirituality with Teilhard de Chardin*. Maryknoll, N.Y.: Orbis Press, 1997.

———. *Spirit of Fire: The Life and Vision of Teilhard de Chardin*. Maryknoll, NY: Orbis Press, 1996.

———. *The Spirit of One Earth: Reflections on Teilhard de Chardin and Global Spirituality*. New York: Paragon House, 1989.

Leonard, William J., SJ. *The Letter Carrier*. Kansas City, MO; Sheed and Ward, 1993.

Lukas, Mary, and Ellen Lukas. *Teilhard*. New York: Doubleday and Company, 1977.

Mooney, Christopher F., SJ. *Teilhard de Chardin and the Mystery of Christ*. New York: Harper and Row, 1964.

Mortier, Jeanne, and Marie-Louise Auboux, eds. *Teilhard de Chardin Album*. New York: Harper and Row, 1966.

Padberg, John W., SJ, ed. *The Constitutions of the Society of Jesus and Their Complementary Norms*. Saint Louis: Institute of Jesuit Sources, 1996.

Quinan, Michael D, OFM. *Job in the Collegeville Bible Commentary*, edited by Dianne Bergant, CSA, and Robert Karris, OFM. Collegeville, MN: Liturgical Press, 1989.

Schmitz-Moormann, Karl, and Nicole Schmitz-Moormann, eds. *Teilhard de Chardin: L'oervres scientifique*. Friburg im Brisgau, Germany: Walter Verlag, 1971.

Skehan, James W., SJ. *Place Me with Your Son: Ignatian Spirituality in Everyday Life*. 3d ed. Washington, D.C.: Georgetown University Press, 1991.

Smith-Moran, Barbara. *Soul at Work: Reflections on Spirituality of Working*. Winona, MN: Saint Mary's Press, 1997.

Teilhard de Chardin, Pierre, SJ. *The Divine Milieu*. New York: Harper and Row, 1960.

———. *The Heart of Matter*. New York: Harcourt Brace and Company, 1950.

———. *Hymn of the Universe*. New York: Harper and Row, 1961, 1965.

———. *Letters from a Traveller*. New York: Harper and Row, 1962.

———. *Letters to Two Friends: 1926–1952*. New York: New American Library, 1968.

———. *The Making of a Mind: Letters from a Soldier-Priest,*

1914–1919. New York: Harper and Row, 1965.

———. *Writings in Time of War*. New York: Harper and Row, 1965.

Acknowledgments *(continued)*

The scriptural quotations are from the New American Bible. Copyright © 1991, 1986, 1970 by the Confraternity of Christian Doctrine, Washington, DC 20017-1194. All rights reserved.

The quotation on page 14 is from *The Spirit of One Earth: Reflections on Teilhard de Chardin and Global Spirituality*, by Ursula King (New York: Paragon House, 1989). Copyright © 1989 by Ursula King.

The quotations on pages 20, 34, 35, 37, 37, 48, 55, 55, 65, 65, 68, 71–72, 72, 78, 78–79, 81, 83, 84, 85, 87, 104, 106–107, 111, 112, 112, 112–113, 116, 116, and 116 are from *The Divine Milieu*, by Pierre Teilhard de Chardin (New York: Harper and Row, 1960). Copyright © 1960 by William Collins Sons and Company, London, and Harper and Row Publishers, Inc., New York. All rights reserved. [Permission applied for.] [British Commonwealth rights applied for.]

The quotations on pages 21, 22, 24, 24, 25, 26, 27, 28, 30, 30, 41, 59, 59, 77, 77, 77–78, 78, 82, 82, 90, and 96 are from *Spirit of Fire: The Life and Vision of Teilhard de Chardin*, by Ursula King (Maryknoll, NY: Orbis Press, 1996). Copyright © 1996 by Ursula King. Used by permission.

The quotations on pages 36, 36–37, 40, 59, 60, 60–61, 69, 76, 80, 82, 92, 92, 92, 92–93, 98, 102, 102, 102, 102–103, 103, 105, 110, 110, 110, 113, and 117 are from *Teilhard de Chardin and the Mystery of Christ*, by Christopher F. Mooney, SJ (New York: Harper and Row, 1964, 1965, 1966). Copyright 1964, 1965, 1966 by Christopher F. Mooney. [Permission applied for.]

The quotations on pages 41, 42, 44, 54, 57, 58, 97, 99, 100, and 101 are from *Hymn of the Universe*, by Pierre Teilhard de Chardin (New York: Harper and Row, 1960). Copyright © 1961 by Editions du Seuil. French copyright: *Hymne à l'univers* by Pierre Teilhard de Chardin © Editions du Seuil, 1961. English translation copyright © 1965 by William Collins Sons and Company, London, and Harper and Row, New York. All rights reserved. Used by permission.

The quotations on pages 46, 58, 59–60, 86, 88, 89, 100–101, 103, 104, 104–105, and 106 are from *Writings in Time of War*, by Pierre Teilhard de Chardin, SJ (New York: Harper and Row, 1965, 1968). Copyright © 1965 by Editions Bernard Grasset. All rights reserved. Used by permission.

Titles in the Companions for the Journey Series

Praying with Anthony of Padua
Praying with Benedict
Praying with C. S. Lewis
Praying with Catherine McAuley
Praying with Catherine of Siena
Praying with the Celtic Saints
Praying with Clare of Assisi
Praying with Dante
Praying with Dominic
Praying with Dorothy Day
Praying with Elizabeth Seton
Praying with Francis of Assisi
Praying with Francis de Sales
Praying with Frédéric Ozanam
Praying with Hildegard of Bingen
Praying with Ignatius of Loyola
Praying with John Baptist de La Salle
Praying with John Cardinal Newman
Praying with John of the Cross
Praying with Julian of Norwich
Praying with Louise de Marillac
Praying with Martin Luther
Praying with Meister Eckhart
Praying with Mother Teresa
Praying with Pope John XXIII
Praying with Teilhard de Chardin
Praying with Teresa of Ávila
Praying with Thérèse of Lisieux
Praying with Thomas Aquinas
Praying with Thomas Merton
Praying with Vincent de Paul

Order from your local religious bookstore or from

Saint Mary's Press
702 Terrace Heights
Winona MN 55987-1320
USA
800-533-8095
www.smp.org